Simple Spells for Love

Simple Spells for Love

ANCIENT PRACTICES
FOR
EMOTIONAL
FULFILLMENT

Barrie Dolnick

Barrie Dolnick

Harmony Books
New York

Published by Harmony Books, a division of Crown Publishers, Inc.,
201 East 50th Street, New York, New York 10022.
Member of the Crown Publishing Group.

Random House, Inc. New York, Toronto, London, Sydney, Auckland

HARMONY and colophon are trademarks of Crown Publishers, Inc.

Manufactured in the United States of America

Design by Linda Kocur

Library of Congress Cataloging-in-Publication Data
Dolnick, Barrie.
Simple spells for love: ancient practices for emotional fulfillment/
by Barrie Dolnick.
1. Magic. 2. Love—Miscellanea. I. Title.
BF1623.L6D65 1995   94-31885
133.4′42—dc20   CIP
ISBN 0-517-79995-2
First Edition

in memory of
Elizabeth Milavsky Friedman

Acknowledgments

I am particularly grateful to the kind teachers I have had in making this book a reality: M. Allethem, Shaye Areheart, Donna Black, Julia Condon, Bruce Harris, Susan Lemak, Glen Maera, Liz Nickles, Marcia Lane Purcell, Emma Sweeney, and Julie Winter.

And to my mother, Sandy Dolnick.

Contents

Preface

You'll have no need of a cauldron, eye of newt, spider tongues, or other such trappings that people traditionally identify with spell casting. Instead, you will find that spells demand integrity, courage, and personal commitment, not to mention patience.

Spells are first cast from within, and that means within you. Only then can they take hold on the outside, and perform the magic you have initiated. Spells are not for the fainthearted.

Prepare yourself for a journey into your mystical side.

> *"Accustom yourself continually*
> *to make many acts of love,*
> *for they enkindle and*
> *melt the soul."*

—*Interior Castle,*
Saint Teresa of Avila

Simple Spells for Love

ONE

introduction to

SPELL
CASTING

$\mathcal{S}$pell casting: not-so-foreign territory

♥

Red roses
Floral perfume
Candles

Casting spells is something you do already. The practice is an unconscious ritual in our society. For instance, when you put on perfume,
you are amplifying your own energy through scent, which can make
you more attractive to others. A gift of red roses is a common love
spell, eliciting passionate energy between you and your loved one. Is
it any wonder that we all take pleasure in the rituals of romance?

Perfume and red roses are clichés, yet such gifts are charged with
ancient significance. Flowers and scents have specific meanings in
folklore, which are linked to practices of magic, such as spell casting.
This is also true of gemstones. The diamond, a common token of
engagement or marriage, is a natural earth crystal that has long
symbolized the divine alliance of mind, body, and spirit that is true
love. These elements work to heighten the senses, which in turn
evoke a deeper, more significant reaction.

Red roses, perfume, diamonds—all are common to the art of
attracting love and keeping love, but these are only the most popular
examples of the many flowers, scents, and stones that can help you
consciously manifest the love you desire. One should also be aware
that use of colors, days of the week, and even hours of the day can
add to your allure and put more spice in your love life.

The use of spells is not at all new; in fact, it is ancient. As we
move toward the millennium, you will see increasing interest in
nature and natural remedies. Spells are like natural remedies, and

the elements you will use in your spells are natural to our planet, and often to your own garden. There is no need for eye of newt, bat wings, spider's webs, or whatever else you may have imagined. Although spells exist that call for such items, they are *not* love spells. And this book is only about love spells.

What is a spell?
♥

In its simplest state, a spell is an organized wish that actually carries with it some power to manifest. *The spell you cast is a conscious direction of energy or influence, which helps increase the likelihood of the outcome you desire.*

The easiest example of an everyday spell is that of a wedding. That ceremony, by tradition, uses all the trappings of a spell and is, in fact, very powerful. The candles, the wine, the flowers—oftentimes orange blossom, a very strong love herb—and especially the vows said aloud, are the main ingredients in many of the spells described in this book. The power of a group added to this ritual makes it a strong spell. We think of weddings as mainly religious ceremonies, but we tend to forget that all religions as we know them are relatively new to the world. For centuries, ancient magic was incorporated into modern religion. Often, what we consider mere ceremony was once sacred ritual.

There are many kinds of spells, and many ways in which to cast them. For the purposes of this book, only white-magic spells are offered; such spells do not interfere with the free will of others. This means that these spells are done in recognition of the greater good; if it is not in your best interest or that of the concerned party, the spell will not take hold. Thus you will be protected from the adverse effects of magic, and can be assured that whomever you desire is an appropriate lover. While you may believe very deeply that a certain person is right for you, the two of you may not be the right match. Sometimes that nicely wrapped package you are eager to open holds a jacket in the wrong size or color. The spells in this book help to ensure that the love you give and the love you hope to receive are a perfect fit.

Elemental magic
♥

Magic, which is the ability to influence events through energetic manipulation, is grounded in the simple elements we rely on in our daily life. It can be defined as the ability to call upon the elements to manifest your desires. Fire, earth, air, and water are the elements we need for our survival. The energy to access, utilize, and organize these elements is what we call magic. In these spells, you will learn how to create the energy—or magic—needed to influence events.

The elements are represented by thousands of symbols in our lives, and you can find every element everywhere you go: fire comes from the sun or from light; water constitutes the greatest part of your body; earth is what you are bound to by gravity; and air is, of course, what you breathe, what surrounds every part of you.

In spells, fire is often represented by a candle. The flame is a symbol of passion, an ardent expression of love. Fire is needed as fuel or impetus to push forward the energy of initiation. Fire is also much relied upon in igniting passions of physical love.

Earth is the element that allows life to take its physical form. It rules the very body you live in, and your connection to the world in general. Earth, which is tactile, fertile, and steady, is important to magic in that it makes your spell manifest in your life as a reality. The symbol for earth is often a candle on which a flame is lit.

Air is the element that represents the thought form—the idea or the wish behind the magic. The realm of air—of thought or intention—is where all things live before they become reality. That is to say, whatever occurs has been thought of in some form, whether conscious or unconscious. Spell casting ensures that your thought form, or wish, is conscious and thorough. Air can be represented by the smoke of a candle or by your own breath when it is used consciously in a spell.

Water is the element most often associated with love, for it is the one that rules emotions. It is a very complicated element: fertile, reproductive, sensual and sexual, deep and uncontained. It is extremely important to love magic when you are casting spells for deeply romantic love. Water can be represented by a bowl or glass of water, or simply by the water in the vessel where flowers are placed.

What are love spells?

♥

Love spells are not psychic personal ads or magical dating services; they do not perform only at your whim, or through sheer will. Good love spells are not manipulative or dangerous, and they are absolutely *not* foolproof. A foolish intention will produce a foolish outcome.

Love spells are a cosmic blueprint that contain your best energetic description of the love you desire. As you become accustomed to the way spells are cast, you'll find the process becomes easier and easier to use.

To make a successful spell, you need to believe in some form of magic. If you have a spiritual belief system, you already have magic in your life. Some call it divine mystery or cosmic flow, but if you are a religious person, it is your idea of God. It doesn't matter what you call your understanding of a higher power than yourself, but it does matter that you believe in *something*. If you are a complete rationalist, an atheist, or a fatalist, you will have little access to the world of magic, and thus your spells probably won't be successful. People who need a rational explanation for everything are afraid of the mysteries of the universe. They can have a hard time with love, too.

Making a spell is similar to asking a great but temperamental chef to make something just for you, after you explain your tastes: hot, cold, salty, sweet, rich, spicy, bland, adventurous, and so on. You have the opportunity to define the qualities you desire, but it is important not to dictate exactly what the dish should look like or what it should be. You can try to request when you'd like it to be ready, but this, too, can offend the chef. You have to trust that what is created for you will be perfectly satisfying. In fact, you may be surprised at what you find pleasing in the end.

The spells in this book will work for all your wishes: for romance, for a mate, for friendship, for acceptance, and even for conception. They can also help in healing a broken heart.

These spells may also work in ways you can't anticipate. As you read through the book, you'll see how unpredictable the process is, which can make it a lot of fun unless you are a controlling personality, in which case you may find the process frustrating. In that case, think of it as an exercise in learning how to let go.

Don't be discouraged if you find that you don't care for the first few dishes that the universe serves up. It often takes a few stabs at manifestation before the fit is right. Think of it as a few appetizers before you're served the main course. In the meantime you may come across a few toads, or be disappointed that the process hasn't produced the results you want. This is a learning process, too. It will work, if you keep the faith. *The more faith you have in the spell you use, the more success you'll have.*

It is important to remember that casting a spell is not an attempt to fill a specific order. Again, let me warn you that you are not using the personal ads. Your spell is most potent when you concentrate on the *nonspecific* physical aspects, but stay with the emotional and sensual requirements. For instance, if you wish to describe the mate you would like, you could include such traits as *loving, affectionate, kind, funny, prosperous, respectful, intelligent, fun-loving, artistic, tender,* or *energetic.*

You will not be as successful with your spell if you ask for specific height, weight, eye color, and so forth, but you can ask for an appropriate match to your sensual needs. You want to find someone attractive, but you may not know exactly how to define it physically. Finding love is not a physical venture; leave that to making love. To find love you must see through your heart, not through your eyes. *Your heart is where you cast your spell.*

In order to cast these spells you must learn where your heart energy comes from. There is a place called your *heart center,* which is located directly in the center of your chest, between your nipples. Place your fingers on this area of your chest. Often this is a tender spot, and, when you get more familiar with it, you'll be able to sense it without touching it. Sometimes when your heart is broken this spot actually hurts. We will be using the heart center in many of our spells, so start tuning in to yours now, just by being conscious of it—how it feels to you, how it may change during the course of your day, or in the company of different people.

Magic and objectivity

♥

A love spell differs from other kinds of spells in that you are using or creating emotional ties with other people. Magic works best in objective situations, when you can remove as much emotion as possible from the spell itself. This is not always possible in love spells, but there are ways to check whether you are investing the wrong kind of emotional energy into your spell. This caution will appear in the instructions prior to each section, and it is strongly advised that you heed it. *Because you are influencing other people with your spell, it is very important that you not tamper with their free will; this is black magic.* It is also important that you not put sticky emotional energy, such as possessiveness, fear, jealousy, or vengefulness, into the spell. As Donna, my friend and avid spell caster, is quick to point out, it will come back and smack you in the head. Whatever you put into a spell you will get back, and sticky emotional energy breeds sticky situations.

Anabel found this out when she used a spell for commitment on a man she had dated only twice. She was fearful that he was going to stop seeing her, and she was tired of rejection. Her spell took hold, and she found herself immersed in a relationship that led quickly to engagement. Unfortunately, fear often acts as a magnet to attract the very behavior one is trying to avoid. Her engagement was broken eventually, because the spell was cast upon an inappropriate man, with fear rather than love as the motivating element. Anabel suffered far more from this broken engagement than she would have from a short-lived dating romance.

Spell requirements: belief, intention, allowing

♥

There is an art to the spell, but it is not complicated. *Belief,* along with *intention* and *allowing,* are the necessary components of spell casting. With all three of these ingredients, and one or two of the recipes in this book, you will be able to cast a successful spell.

As with many magic practices, it becomes easier and is most effective when there is real belief behind it. You will find that your belief grows as your success with spells becomes apparent. Sometimes, even in magic, seeing is believing.

Believe it

In the stage version of J. M. Barrie's *Peter Pan,* there is a scene in which the fairy Tinkerbell, represented by a small, fading light, is dying. She can be saved only by the audience, who must clap their hands to show that they believe in fairies. As the applause swells, her light grows brighter, and Tinkerbell lives. Though it may be a childish example, this is the clearest way to define how a spell works. You must *believe* in your spell for it to have life.

Inventors and entrepreneurs know this. They are the magicians of our time. They believe in the possibility of things that do not yet exist, and they have the courage to take the risks that can make them a reality. You can be an entrepreneur in the world of love as you learn to cast your spells.

You can still be a skeptic, too. In this scientific age, the idea of magic probably seems odd at first. You may raise your eyebrows at some of the instructions you'll be given. That's okay, as long as you can put aside your doubts long enough to let yourself believe in the power of the spell you're using.

You may need to find the room to be an innocent again, childlike in the possibilities of the world. If you can muster this awe and openness within yourself, you can probably find the belief you need for your spell to do its work.

If *you* don't believe in your own spell, how can it possibly work for you and someone else?

Intention: be open to possibilities

There is a fine line between the magic of *intention* and the sheer energy of *will.* There is an old saying in our culture, "Where there's a will, there's a way." In spell casting, this does *not* hold true.

The difference between intention and will is the amount of space that you leave for your spell to perform its magic. Will is rather narrow and may not allow all the possibilities of the spell to manifest. Spells are weakened when one tries to control their outcomes exactly, such as "I want a six-foot-two, athletic lawyer with blue eyes and dark hair."

Here's where dating through personal ads can go wrong. Tom, an investment banker, said he'd met a lot of nice women as a result of his ad, but while they met his physical requirements on paper, they weren't close to the sparkling, sensual, interesting woman of his dreams. If he had cast a spell instead, he would have used his heart and not his head. He probably would have had better luck.

If you request an appropriate partner with the qualities you desire—such as kindness, humor, and patience—you'll probably get better results and a nicer mate.

Intention is more malleable than will, and it focuses on the general outcome rather than on specifics. This allows your spell to weave and manifest more options than you would have thought possible.

For example, Diane was ready for marriage after six years of the dating scene and one serious relationship. Her vision of the right man had something to do with a white-collar executive and lots of money, not to mention dashing looks. Nonetheless, Diane managed to put aside this stereotype and proceeded to cast a spell.

Using a spell to attract men, she added a marriageability factor to her general attraction spell. She went about her life as usual, and was surprised by the variety of men who began to show up. She was tickled that the plumber who came to unclog her bathtub drain asked her for a date, but she did not accept. Nor did she want to date the policeman who lived next door. However, she met a man as she stood having her skirt hemmed at her tailor's. He chatted with her while he waited for his clothes, and left, after having written his name and number on an order form and slipped it into her jacket pocket when she wasn't looking. She thought he was attractive but poor; he had been wearing crummy jeans and a grungy shirt, and had paid for his clothes in crumpled cash.

Even though he didn't *look* like marriage material, she went with her impulse. Upon finding his phone number in her pocket, she called him up. He was delighted that she took him up on his overture, and, many dates later, they married. His grungy clothing was typical of an associate professor at a nearby college. He wasn't her white-collar man, but to her surprise, he was just right. As it turned out, he had a prosperous and interesting future.

Diane managed to keep her *intention* going without imposing her will onto her spell. If she hadn't been open to the possibilities beyond her own conception of the right man, she would not have met her husband.

Allowing

The art of *allowing* is linked to intention, but it requires relaxing the desire to control the outcome of a process.

Lynn, a twice-divorced thirty-nine-year-old woman, was not familiar with the modern dating scene. She cast a spell to help her attract men, which, in the city where she lived, seemed to be a far-fetched idea. While she had her doubts concerning the kind of men who were available, she cast her spell and waited to see just who would show up.

After two months of keeping an eye out for a new man in her life, the only one Lynn was attracted to was her aerobics instructor, whose preference was for his own sex. Even though Lynn knew that he was not dating material, seeing him motivated her to exercise more, which enhanced her appearance and built her confidence. She began to wear more flattering clothes and changed her hair and makeup. Still, tired of waiting, Lynn gave up on her spell.

Lynn's new boyfriend seemingly came out of nowhere. About ten weeks after she cast her spell, Lynn and a girlfriend popped into a bar on a whim, after an early movie. There was a band playing the Lambada, and by the end of the night, Lynn was in a passionate embrace with her dance partner, who became her boyfriend. By giving up on her spell, she actually released control, and got results.

To create successful spells, you have to give up control, yet you still have to participate in the process. Even though you can't say how it will work, you have to work *with* it. This is called "putting legs on it." If Lynn had just stayed home, waiting for the phone to ring, she wouldn't have gotten anywhere. She participated in her spell by making herself available to meet men. She did what she could to give her spell a chance to take hold, but still she had to allow it to work.

Bob, a twenty-five-year-old man, cast a spell and made a charm to attract women. He carried the charm with him every day in his pocket. He also asked all of his friends to set him up with any blind dates they thought would be appropriate. Bob had five or six such dates, none of which were right for him. He didn't find this depressing, however, since he looked at each one as an opportunity to practice for the right one. His new girlfriend, as it turned out, showed up by looking into his mouth. His dental hygienist flirted with him, and he found himself asking her out, something he would not have done easily before all of his practice dates. Although he had become only marginally conscious of having it with him, he also had the confidence his charm gave him. The charm had become part of his normal pocket junk.

Allowing is the process of letting your spell work. Once you can let go, the divine chaos of magic can throw you a few bouquets.

Checklist for spell casting

1. Do you believe in your spell and in your ability to conjure what you want?

2. Are you focused on an outcome? Have you room for possibilities beyond what you can imagine?

3. Are you able to allow the process to take place? Can you see yourself participating in your own spell?

If you can answer *yes* to all of the above, you are ready to create magic.

The primary spell
♥

Each area of spell casting includes a Primary Spell that functions as the basis of your effort. The Primary Spell must be observed carefully. This is where you lay your groundwork, and if you intend to get results, you must take this spell seriously.

Other spells
♥

For each chapter, there are other spells you may cast in addition to the Primary Spell. You may do as many of these spells as you like, but avoid the unnecessary. Your magic won't work well if you give it too many directions.

Within the additional spells, you may be more creative than with the Primary Spell; if you want to add your own touches to them, you have the freedom to do so. Some people like to play favorite love songs when performing spells; others like to dress in silky robes. You may put your personal touch onto these spells, as long as you maintain some of the elements that are suggested here. Spell casting is a highly personal task, and after you have mastered the basics, you will probably want to add a lot of your own ideas.

How to find what you need: spell ingredients
♥

Many of the ingredients involved in spell casting will be readily available to you. You will need to know a reasonable florist or flower market. Candles are accessible in many household-goods stores, card shops, and variety stores. If you choose to use jewels or crystals, you can make use of whatever you own, or you can buy small stones. Even if your spell requires a ruby or a garnet, you needn't spend a lot of money on anything. The stone, *in any form,* generates the power you'll need. You may want to investigate the crystal shop or New Age bookstore in your area. Many carry most of the objects you will require, and if yours doesn't, someone who works there will usually know where you can find them.

For more obscure herbs, roots, and scents, look for a botanica or a natural foods outlet. Botanicas are common in Hispanic neighborhoods, and are the best resources for spell ingredients. Many have their own love incenses, sachets, charms, and scents. You can use these if you like, but you are encouraged to do your own thing wherever possible. Doing so increases the personal power behind your spell, making your results more suitable for you. Natural food stores and places that sell natural health products will also have many of the ingredients you'll need.

The essentials of timing
♥

Moon phases
Perhaps the most overlooked but powerful cycle in our culture is that of the Moon. We seem to think that the ancients, who used the full Moon to signify market days, did so only because they lacked a

real calendar or quartz watches. We underestimate our ancestors. They understood the importance of the lunar cycle, which is not only essential to life, but is absolutely critical to spell casting.

Never cast a love spell when the Moon is waning—that is, after it's past full and fading to new.

In the most literal interpretation, the Moon, when it is full or growing toward full, serves as a metaphor, a signal for when it is good and appropriate to build or manifest. When the Moon is diminishing, the power of manifestation decreases with it.

For those who use a more abstract and ethereal interpretation, the Moon is the power of manifestation. In astrology, it signifies fertility and sexuality, as well as the emotional side of life. The Moon is one of the heavenly bodies that rule love. When the Moon is growing to full, the potential for love increases. When it is fading, its power to manifest love fades with it. In fact, as the Moon falls away to renew itself, it is a good time to ask for things to be taken away. For example, if you want to break up with someone, the waning Moon will serve you.

The Moon has a powerful effect on the earth's tides, weather, and other phenomena, and it is physically, psychically, and emotionally influential in the lives of human beings. You'll begin to realize the significance of the Moon's cycles when you follow the instructions for your desired spell. Wait for the Moon to be right for the spell you've chosen. Weather reports and many calendars include the cycles of the Moon.

Planetary days and hours
Ancient knowledge used in spell casting gives significance to the hours of the day and to the days of the week.

In some cases, the names of the days of the week still sound like the planets they represent:

SUNDAY. THE SUN: power, friendship, healing

MONDAY. THE MOON: fertility, emotions, domesticity

TUESDAY. MARS: aggression, passion, courage

WEDNESDAY. MERCURY: communications, travel, learning

THURSDAY. JUPITER: expansiveness, prosperity, adventure

FRIDAY. VENUS: relationships, love, pleasure

SATURDAY. SATURN: contraction, practicality, limitations

Planets that are love-friendly are the Moon, Jupiter, and Venus. For men, Mars can work for certain spells to attract women. On Sunday, the Sun's happy day, just lie back and enjoy life. Saturn-ruled Saturday is best for practical efforts. It is strange that what has traditionally been "date night" is actually not the best day for it. If you want to stack the deck for a good time, go out on a Thursday or Friday.

Certain hours are best for spell casting. Without exception, these are the hours of the night, since all magic is most powerful in the darkness. You can increase the power of your spell by casting it on the right day and in the right hour of the night. Pay attention to the hour that is recommended for the casting of each spell.

These spells work

♥

As a constant spell caster, I can attest to their effectiveness. They really do work, and in ways that you will not be able to predict.

The more powerful the spell, the more dramatic the results. Sometimes the results may seem like setbacks at first. This is not uncommon. If you are trying to attract new love in your life, you may have to resolve a past relationship first. If you are trying to have a baby, you may have to address some hidden fears of childbearing before you get pregnant. Spells can work in weird ways, and it is possible that seemingly negative events will take place initially. Usually, when this happens, it is a necessary clearing of the past, so that you can move on to what you desire. Sometimes it takes hindsight to understand this, just as Lynn found. Her spell increased her self-esteem, which ultimately brought her a new lover.

When the spell takes hold in the direction you want it to, hold on to your hat. If you put a lot of power into your spell, you can get some impressive results. My own experience comes to mind. Using a spell to attract a new lover at a time when I was not in a relationship, I went to a party where I met two men, each of whom walked me into the moonlight and kissed me. The next day I ran into an old beau, and ended up in a passionate embrace with him that evening. I met two more men within that week. I was excited and exhausted. I hadn't expected the spell to work so quickly or so powerfully. Brace yourself. It is a lot of fun, but you have to have the room in your life to enjoy it.

$\mathscr{A}$ word on charms, glamours, and atmospheres
♥

Before you go off to test your skills in the realm of magic, it is important that you understand the definitions used in the spell-binding processes.

In making *charms*, a material object is "energetically charged" with certain powers. Some people carry a rabbit's foot, some have a lucky tie. In *The Wizard of Oz*, Dorothy had her slippers. They all have one thing in common: a belief that the item is endowed with a power that can influence events. Charms work, and if you charge them well, they work very well. This book will give you various opportunities to make charms to use for your efforts in love.

A *glamour*, on the other hand, is like a cloak of energy that conceals or protects an individual's identity. If you feel less than confident about your looks or your magnetism, a glamour can lift the energy around you so that people see you the way you'd like to be seen. Glamours work well when you feel insecure but still have the desire to appear in a social setting. A glamour is even useful when you feel fat or when you're having a "bad hair day" and you want to look better.

An *atmosphere* is what one creates to directly influence the energy of a physical place. For example, you can manipulate the actual atmosphere of a space, such as a room, a house, or an apartment, to make it either more or less hospitable to those inside it. Creating an atmosphere is extremely useful when entertaining. You already know the romantic cliché of candlelight and music; doing it within a spell gives it a real spin. Casting an atmosphere is also excellent for giving parties, when you want to create a lot of fun, or even just a relaxed evening.

In the chapter on spells for attraction, you will also learn about casting your personal atmosphere, which deals with the kind of energy you emit unconsciously. If you are at all unsure about how other people perceive you, then this technique will give you some confidence.

TWO

GENERAL
LOVE
SPELLS

Love is emotion in its purest form, and to some, love is the essence of God or Spirit. Whatever your belief is about love, there are many ways you can express it and many ways to enjoy it. It is both foolish and cruel to restrict the amount of love you have in your life, whether you are focused on giving love or receiving it, or placing yourself within the blessed balance of the two. Love is honorable, dignified, simple, and divine. We spend far too much time trying to figure it out and not nearly enough time participating in it.

Love is not a commodity. Love is not rationed, it is not limited, and it is not something that should be jealously guarded.

Most of the spells in this book address the subject of romantic love, but there are many more kinds of love. To be *in love* with someone is not the same as *loving* someone. You can love your dog as much as your lover, but you'll be quick to point out that those two kinds of love are expressed in entirely different ways.

Your capacity to love is endless. It can be as large or as limited as you decide. Most agree that feeling love, whether in giving or receiving, is highly pleasurable and rewarding. If you want to increase the amount of pleasure in your life, you may like to cast spells for love in general. Love is not just partnership; the more you practice with love and clear your access to love, the more love is available to you.

Love is not without its risks, however. You may find it hard to open yourself to loving because you are afraid of the responsibility and the risk of hurt. There is no guarantee that you won't feel pain or cause pain in your quest for love. You may get hurt; you may hurt someone else. This is part of the experience. You don't have to be devastated, and you don't have to cause pain recklessly. The pleasure of love can and usually does outweigh the risk of pain. Fear of pain will be a very dull jail cell if you allow it to rule your life. You may not get hurt if you don't love, but you certainly won't feel love's great pleasure, either.

The spells in this chapter will give you basic tools to increase the love in your life, including a few spells to clear the fear of pain. From my own experiences, I feel great sadness for those people who bury their lives with work and do not allow themselves to play with love. They see love as frivolous and time-wasting. What pleasure they miss, and how hard life must feel without love.

Love doesn't have to mean romantic love or naturally lead to marriage. It can be love for an animal, a family member, even an old friend. Any love is worthwhile. All love amplifies your life in tangible and intangible ways, enriching your experience and giving you a depth that contributes to all parts of your life: health, work, prosperity, creativity, spirituality . . . the list is endless.

Clearing the path for love
♥

As mentioned previously, many of us have experienced the pain that often accompanies love. From the recent public unveilings of childhood abuse, both physical and emotional, we are now more familiar with how lack of love affects our behavior as adults. A profusion of talk shows and self-help books show us how our early experiences inform our current ones unless we free ourselves from negative patterns. Sometimes this takes therapy; sometimes it's a matter of undergoing a few negative experiences as an adult until you realize what in yourself needs to be changed. Not all of us have an aversion to love or negative patterns associated with it, but, oddly, the majority of us do.

If you are sincerely open to the process, you can address and release your fears or aversions to love through spell casting. Spells can act very strongly when you are unearthing fears and negative patterns because you are working within the framework of the greater good, and there is no stronger pull to the greater good than unleashing the fear that prevents you from living in the flow of life, which is the flow of love. In spell making, it is important to be clear about your emotions and to allow your fears to rise, be recognized, and claimed, so that they release their hold on you. This is why spell casting is particularly good at cleansing fear; it is natural to the process.

Since clearing the path toward love can and usually does bring up fears reminiscent of previous bad experiences, it is important to follow the steps to this spell carefully. If you are too lax in your spell casting, you can bring about an abrupt clearing, which can be an emotionally draining experience.

At times I have little patience for this process, and I can attest to the power of the clearing spell. It can be used at any time, for any situation that has caused you to feel some unpleasantness or residual anger. In my case, I felt betrayed by a friend at work, and I couldn't forgive her for her unintentional act that had caused me embarrassment and humiliation. I was hurt, because we had been excellent friends for years. We had seen each other through many difficult situations, yet she had done something that caused me a great deal of pain. The situation was awkward at best, and I couldn't find it in myself to even approach her about the subject.

I cast a spell for clearing the path, thinking that it was a simple task and that the spell wouldn't need much time to work. I rushed through it instead of taking the time required. The effects of the spell rendered me almost unsocialized. The anger that consumed me was remarkable; I couldn't get up in the morning without being in a rage. I had unleashed more than I had bargained for, opening up a well of past betrayals unrelated to this incident. In addition to my anger, I felt a great deal of sadness. It took me a week to return to normal. I really had to watch my tongue all that week, afraid that I would say something harsh to my coworkers, family, or friends. I deemed myself unfit for society and didn't socialize at all until the clearing ceased. After this overdramatic reaction, I was able to approach my friend, calmly explain my feelings of betrayal, and receive a heartfelt apology. Whatever had hurt me so much had dissipated with the rest of my rage and pain. We were friends again and, more important, there was a new depth to our friendship and increased respect for each other's feelings, which is all you can ask for in any love relationship.

Clearing the way for love can be used simply to open yourself up to love in your life or for a specific situation as described above. This is a ritual that can be used over and over again in your life to bring about deeper commitments and pleasures.

Uh-oh, accountability

♥

Rats. It isn't just the other person's fault. Ever. By generating love in any way—romantic, familial, platonic, animal, etc.—you are accountable for your participation in the relationship you have fostered. This does not mean that it is your fault when things don't work out, but that there really isn't any fault, for anyone. You have chosen to be in a relationship, so it is your responsibility to deal with it.

The adage that "you can choose your friends but you can't choose your family" doesn't apply here. You can choose how you deal with your family, as much as you can choose whom you deal with as your friends, your coworkers, or acquaintances. No individual is ever entirely at fault in the problems of relationships and love; the burden is always shared. The rest of this chapter will provide examples of how you can work with your accountability. You can learn a lot about both yourself and the people you love when you take the approach that you're in this together.

Love yourself first

♥

You truly do have to love yourself first. This is not to say that you should be a rampant egotist. It is a simple matter of appreciating your own ability to love and be loved. It is difficult if not impossible to be loved when you are full of self-loathing, because you aren't able to feel any love that is offered.

If you are one of those people who turn anger inward, you'll probably need to use the spell for self-love as well as the spell for clearing the path to love. It is not life-enhancing to hate any part of yourself. Conversely, it is very energizing to love and honor what you have been given in this life: your body, your mind, your creativity, and so on. The more you recognize your own gifts, the more others will see them too. Much of this requires the adjustment of your attitude to a positive and hence attractive outlook. If you like yourself, others will too.

Maggie had a problem with her body. She felt fat, when in fact she was not at all overweight. She saw her large breasts as enemies, making her look heavy on top. Although her waist was small, she hated her wide hips, and despaired whenever she tried on clothes. She hated the way things looked on her, so she tended to wear clothes that were too big on her just to avoid feeling fat—yet she still didn't feel attractive.

When Maggie's employer transferred her to another city, she cast a spell to attract love. When it didn't work, she tried a spell to clear the path for love instead. She felt her old anxiety and self-loathing rise in her body as she was casting her spell. While she was waiting for her spell to work, she concentrated on fixing up her new apartment. Maria, a friendly woman from her new office, offered to help Maggie shop for curtains. Maria was also a clotheshorse and an avid shopper who took Maggie to a few of her favorite stores. Maria's enthusiasm led Maggie to try on a red dress with a low-cut neckline and a cinched waist. Maggie was embarrassed to come out of the dressing room to show Maria how it looked, but she held her breath, conscious of her cleavage and her obvious curving hips, and walked out. Maria raved. She begged Maggie to buy the dress, telling her how fantastic it looked on her and how she wished she had Maggie's figure. Maggie was swept into the thrill of this new appreciation, bought the dress, and tried it on ten times after she got home. Her new attitude toward her body brought out gratitude for her strong feminine shape rather than hatred for unwanted curves. Maggie started dressing in a whole new way, and her path to love opened up. Maria has become a close friend, along with other people Maggie has met. Now that she's comfortable with herself, Maggie is a lot more open to others, romantic prospects included.

Self-love isn't just about the physical part of you. You have more than that to offer. Do you think you're funny or clever? Are you just a nice, relaxed person? Are you a great risk taker? An intellect? A sport? A partyer? There are many dimensions to you. All of them are valuable, all of them worthwhile. Take an inventory. The more you like, the more success you will have with love spells.

Spells to increase love in your life

♥

These spells increase the presence of love in your life with the exception of romantic love, which is covered extensively in subsequent chapters. These spells are better for platonic relationships, familial love, love within the workplace, universal love, and spiritual love.

You may think that you don't need to open up to any more love; your life is full, you can't take any more people, friends, or relationships, but, believe me, you can still benefit from these spells. If you're feeling "maxed out," these spells can give you more room simply by reminding you of the spaciousness that love brings to you. Not every love relationship demands time and nurturing. When you feel as if there is no room for any more love in your life, it is time to be grateful for the love you do have. Gratitude adds spaciousness and a sense of blessedness.

Family love: housework

♥

Family relationships demand a lot of attention, and a general love spell can come in very handy. You can diffuse emotionally charged atmospheres or protect yourself against negative energy while still maintaining compassion and feeling love for the individuals who tend to cause you pain—or at least you can try. These aren't spells for sainthood, however. You won't be able to distance yourself from your feelings, you'll just be able to manage them better, and consequently become more skillful in other, nonfamilial relationships.

Joanie used a spell for protection when she went to visit her mother. She loved her mother, but her ulcer always acted up when she spent a lot of time with her. She almost always had to take her prescription medicine during a visit. Her ulcer rarely bothered her at other times. Joanie reasoned that a spell to shield her from this toxic energy would be a good way to deal with the situation, because she couldn't bring herself to tell her mother directly that she was the problem. In addition to her spell for protection, Joanie made a charm to ground negative energy so that it wouldn't go straight into her. She found that the next visit to her mother was completely different, in part because there were other people around who kept her mother busy. Not only did she avoid getting sick, but she also enjoyed herself, talking to her mother's friends and doing things on her own. She still doesn't know if it was the spell or just luck, but now she won't visit her mother without this new ritual.

There are other instances where general love spells are useful within families, particularly when you are on the outs with a sibling, a parent, or someone else you are close to but can't forgive. The energy of a general love spell is soft and diffuse, which in turn softens you and your attitude when you're around those you love. If you are going into a confrontational situation, both the charm to ground negativity and a general love spell can be very effective. The charm will protect you and the general love spell will open you up to the healing possibilities. Often, when fear or anger are present, you won't be able to see beyond the black-and-white of a situation. This spell can help you find the many gray areas that do exist.

Jerome was frustrated because his brother and equal partner, Barry, wouldn't even discuss the state of the family business they ran together. As financial officer, Jerome needed to make some decisions about their accounting methods, but couldn't make a move without Barry's cooperation. There were many details to go over, but Barry, who traveled quite a bit for the business, wasn't making time to do it. Jerome thought that Barry was avoiding his responsibility, and old sibling rivalries surfaced. Eventually they weren't speaking, the business was in jeopardy of closing, and Jerome threatened a lawsuit to get Barry to either pay attention to the work or to have him removed from his position. Both brothers felt betrayed. Jerome had heard from others about success with spell magic, and decided to try a spell. Under his anger and resentment, he still loved his brother and wanted to find a way to work things out. Jerome needed a spell for clearing the path and a spell for forgiveness. He knew that he had to overcome his own anger before he could talk to his brother again; otherwise they'd still end up fighting bitterly.

Jerome did his spell ritual under a waning Moon, to diminish his own negativity (clearing), and waited for the new Moon to initiate the healing process. After he felt comfortably calm, he cast the spell for healing and a general love spell. He approached his brother casually, calling him on the phone at home. To his surprise, Barry wasn't angry or aggressive. In fact, he expressed his gratitude to Jerome for making the first move, and agreed that they really needed to talk things out. It didn't take long for them to realize that they hadn't been communicating well, and that each had misunderstood the other's motives. As their understanding grew, they found an easy compromise: they would hire an outside consultant to deal with the accounting procedure and allow Jerome to make the final decisions. Barry had no interest in it, and was delighted that Jerome didn't mind looking after those issues. Jerome was relieved to have some of the work taken off his shoulders and to have another person's opinion to help him sort out the issues. They saved their business and, most important, their relationship.

When these spells are cast around family members, they usually work extremely well and very quickly. The reason is obvious: you are most energetically linked to your immediate family. Even though you may be very different from your siblings, your parents, or your cousins, your magic will still take hold easily when you direct it within your circle. You all come from the same source, and you are linked physically, emotionally, and psychically. This is also why it is very important to heal the relationships within your family. Family wounds are always shared among the whole family, even if you think that you have more than your share.

Family acceptance of outsiders
♥

How often have you heard people complain that their families won't accept their lovers, spouses, or friends? It happens all the time, and if you are sensitive to your family's opinions, this can hurt.

Spells can be used to facilitate acceptance, but such a spell is one removed from its maker, and therefore it is not a strong one, by nature. If you hope to help other people find love within themselves, which is basically what you are doing, you may not have as much success as with a spell to love yourself; this is because you cannot control how open others will be. You can only affect your *own* openness, which helps, but does not have a direct effect on those around you.

If you want to get your parents to accept the person you've chosen to marry, for instance, you can cast a general spell for love around you. This can help you feel loved throughout the introduction and evaluating process, so that you may not care whether or not approval is being given. You can also make a charm for you and your intended, to help attract love and friendship, but again, your lover must be open to this idea or it won't work.

My friend April had a real fear of her parents' meeting her prospective in-laws for the first time. She and her fiancé were from similar backgrounds, but the two families' politics were extremely polarized. She saw it as right versus left, and knowing how much her father loved to hear his own voice, she dreaded what she thought would be an unavoidable clash of beliefs. Her fiancé, Chad, was not nearly as worried, and didn't really care who liked whom. It meant a lot to April, however, since she was the one making all the wedding arrangements.

In an effort to help things along, April cast a simple spell for general love, using photographs of each of the parents to have them symbolically present. She cast the spell to surround her own experience of them with love. Less than two weeks later, April's father mentioned that Chad's father had called to ask him to lunch, just to get acquainted. April automatically held her breath, but her father went on to tell her what a nice man he thought Chad's father was, and how they had already established a common interest: they were both golfers and were planning to set a date for eighteen holes. Nothing else was said, and April didn't know what to think. At least there wasn't any initial antipathy. As it turned out, the in-laws got on very well, no politics were discussed, and the wedding plans progressed without unnecessary tension. April forgot that she had ever been worried. Her spell contributed to her well-being and created the space for a nonpartisan relationship to develop between the in-laws.

Love at work
♥

This is going to be a new idea for many of you. You may make friends at work, but how much *love* do you feel? Mary Tyler Moore's character Mary Richards found profound love in the WJM newsroom, where her coworkers became her friends and an important source of support and acceptance.

You may have the good fortune to work in an environment that already provides you with a sense of well-being. Chances are, however, that you don't. Family dysfunctions carry over into the workplace, and any other place where you are together with people for an extended period of time. It takes a pretty special group of people to make the workplace a source of love.

It can be done. You can enhance your own experience at work with these spells, and, in turn, you can learn a lot about yourself.

All relationships—romantic, familial, and platonic—serve us as mirrors for ourselves. Good relationships show us how well balanced we are. It's those sticky relationships that provide the real learning. "Sticky" is a nice way of characterizing the ones that are a pain in the neck. You can find these in your family, but you'll most often find one or two (at least) at work. Those petty tyrants, as Carlos Castaneda calls them, seem to make your life miserable. In fact, they provide a real challenge for you. How can you possibly love the person that won't let you take Friday off? Or how can you find human compassion for the idiot who made such a dreadful error in judgment that it put your whole reputation at risk? Aha. A tough one, but not impossible.

Look in the mirror. Is the problem with the people around you, or are they merely reflecting the dislike you feel for your own weaknesses?

I have a hard time tolerating people who don't get on with the task at hand. I don't procrastinate, and I found that I actively disliked people who did, even if their actions did not affect me. Somehow, procrastination pressed my intolerance button, so I took a moment to look within myself, and eventually I realized that I was reacting to my own fear that the job wouldn't get done and that somehow it would be my fault. When I realized this, I divorced myself from the irrational feeling of responsibility, and it became easier. It wasn't my problem, but somehow, unconsciously, I made it my responsibility. This is an example of a sticky but unnecessary control issue, and like most uncomfortable issues that come up more than once or twice, one just gets better at dealing with it. We all have a lot of sticky issues, by the way. Have you looked at your own?

Some of us dislike people who don't get worked up about problems. My friend Lee used to complain that his assistant never got upset when things went wrong. I found this amusing, since one ought to remain calm when there's a crisis. I pointed this out to Lee, but he still worried that his assistant didn't take things seriously. Because there was a lot of resentment in Lee's attitude, I gave him the spell for clearing first. Afterward, Lee was less angry and talked the issue out with the assistant, who explained that his father was a martinet who didn't allow reaction of any kind in the face of pain or panic. Eventually, Lee began to trust his assistant and other subordinates more. His own reactions to problems have become less dramatic as his trust in his support system has grown. Trust comes with a general sense of love, and makes work a much nicer place.

General spells for love can also help you attract places to work that will be supportive—places where, even if there are interpersonal problems, they can be solved. Eventually these problems help to open you up to more love.

Jane worked for an alcoholic boss, who was by turn lavish with praise and a raging madman out for blood. His rages were not based on performance or personality; he just lashed out arbitrarily. Jane learned a lot from this. At first she was scared of him, and avoided him when she could sense a storm was in the air. It scared her to her core, and she felt that his rage directed at her would be akin to annihilation. Jane tried a charm for protection from negativity and carried it with her faithfully at work. As she relaxed, knowing that her charm was protecting her, Jane went about her job self-consciously. Late one afternoon, as she was on her way to the ladies' room, Jane got pulled into his office and received the full-blown venom of her boss's alcohol-induced rampage. There was no talking back and no avoiding it. While he was letting off steam, Jane was desperately trying to control her bladder. She finally had to get up and leave to go relieve herself. He was still raging when she returned, and somehow the humor of the situation hit her. It was so absurd to think that she'd go back in for another round with her boss. Instead, she just went back to her office and did her work. Eventually he stopped, and, like most of his storms, it blew over.

Jane left that job because she didn't want to work for such a messed-up person. She learned to distance herself from the fear of this boss figure, and was finally able to see him for the sad, sick person he was. She also learned that she had a choice of where she worked and that she could determine the level of abuse that she would not tolerate. On the whole, her boss, the petty tyrant, taught Jane quite a bit about herself. Sometimes this is love at work.

Gratitude
♥

Before you get on with manifesting more love in your life, be sure to stop and give gratitude for what you do have. You can be grateful that you have the love of your friends, your animals, whomever. Gratitude for the love in your life reinforces the depth of that love and makes it that much more precious.

Acknowledging the love you *do* have doesn't mean that you won't get more. Gratitude is a little like a "love magnet." When you have some sort of understanding of how much people mean to you and how much you mean to them, you'll have a clean connection that will help you through whatever pain or hard times you may encounter in life. When someone close to you goes away, by relocating or in death, your grief at this loss will not be weighted down by the unfinished business of love taken for granted. If you have expressed your love for them and you hold their love for you with gratitude, the loss of someone can be less painful. This may sound simplistic, but in this genuine respect for love, there is much joy, satisfaction, and healing.

spell basics

♥

These are the basic ingredients for general love spells, and you may use these components for your own spells once you learn the basics from those in this book.

general love spells

COLOR: Pink

FLOWER: Pink roses

HERB: Lavender

CRYSTAL: Rose quartz

DAY OF THE WEEK: Friday

TIME OF THE DAY: Second hour after sunset

TIME OF THE MONTH: Waxing Moon

clearing the path for love

COLOR: Purple

FLOWER: White carnation

HERB: Bay leaf

DAY OF THE WEEK: Monday

TIME OF THE DAY: First hour after sunset

TIME OF THE MONTH: Waning Moon

primary spell
FOR LOVE

On a Friday during a waxing Moon,
in the second hour after sunset:

Light a pink candle and place
a vase with pink roses in water next to it.

In a natural vessel, such as a shell,
place dried lavender and a piece of rose quartz.
Holding this vessel, face the candle.

SAY ALOUD:
I raise my voice to the Goddess Venus and
the power of the Sun
to manifest love in my life.
I affirm that I am open to love
and that I have much love to give.
I offer my faith in the greater good
that the love that comes to me is seen and honored.
I release this with the power of the Universe and
the power of my own dignity and say
So be it.
And so it is.

spell for clearing the path
TO LOVE

On a Monday under a waning Moon,
during the first hour after sunset:

Light a purple candle and a white candle.
Place a white carnation, a bay leaf, and
a bowl of salt water in front of the candles.

Sit quietly, breathing in and out deeply.
With every intake of breath, breathe in the light of the candles.
With every exhalation, breathe out fears or blockages
that keep you from the love you want.

SAY ALOUD:
I clear myself of the negativity
that impedes me from recognizing the love around me.
I am open and light, I use the fire to purify,
the earth to heal, the air to know,
and the water to cleanse.
I gently release the tangles, the chains, the bonds.
I am free to love and be loved.
With divine energy and blessing,

I say

So be it.

And so it is.

spell for

HEALING AND FORGIVENESS

On a Friday during a waning Moon,
in the fifth hour of darkness:

Light a white candle and a pink candle.
Burn incense of cedar, sandalwood, or cinnamon.
Place some lavender and a glass of water before the candles.

SAY ALOUD:
I gather the powers of the elements
to create the space for healing and forgiveness
in my relationship with _____.
I claim my accountability and my compassion.
I affirm that the highest power embraces us all.
This is done within the greater good and with love.

I say
So be it.
And so it is.

Splash water on the palms of each hand,
on your face, and on your heart center.
Blow the candles out.
Let the incense burn out.

Throw the lavender out when the Moon is new.

spell for
SELF-LOVE

On a Sunday during a waxing Moon,
in the fourth hour of darkness:

Light a white candle and another candle of
your favorite color.
Place a pink rose in a vase of water next to the candles.
Place two halves of an apple before the candles.

Sit quietly before the candles.
Feel yourself surrounded by pink light.
Breathe the light.

Take one half of the apple in your right hand.
Pass the apple into your left hand.

SAY ALOUD:
I honor and love myself as a whole being.
I take delight in myself and I affirm
there is much love within me.

Eat the half of the apple in your hand.
Leave the other half as an offering until the Moon is full.

Blow out the candles.

charm for protection from
NEGATIVE ENERGY

On a Saturday during a waxing Moon,
in the third hour of darkness:

Light a white candle.

Place within a circle of blue cotton cloth:
a piece of onyx, any size
4 peppercorns
a pinch of salt
a sprinkle of lemon juice
Gather the cloth up and secure it
with white thread wound at least
four times around to close the charm.
Hold the charm before the flame.

SAY ALOUD:
I witness and proclaim this charm
as the unity of elemental power and protection.
Within the force of the greater good,
this charm serves to protect me.
I bless its power and offer gratitude for the service it performs.
So be it.
And so it is.

charm to
ATTRACT LOVE

On a Friday during a waxing Moon,
in the second hour of darkness:

Light a pink candle.

Place within a circle of pink cotton cloth:
4 pink rose petals
a small piece of rose quartz
a pinch of lavender
a piece of ginger root
Gather up the circle of cloth
and hold before the flame.

SAY ALOUD:
I call in the elements
and the Goddess Venus to charge this charm
to attract love in the ways most appropriate.
I offer my blessings and gratitude
for all love in my life and say
So be it.
And so it is.

spell of gratitude
FOR LOVE

On a Friday during a waxing Moon,
in the third hour of darkness:

Light four small votive candles,
red, green, purple, and white.
Place your favorite flowers in a vase next to the candles.

SAY ALOUD:
To the guardians of the elements,
to the Goddess,
and to the Universe
I offer my gratitude for the love
that has been created and thrives
in my life.
I honor and respect this love
and welcome more as it grows.
With thanks and blessing
I release this and say
So be it.
And so it is.

THREE

SPELLS FOR ATTRACTING A LOVER

Spells for attraction
♥

Spells for attraction are divided into two main categories. The first category of spells focuses on drawing in potential romantic prospects. This is a necessary first step if you're in a starting position—that is, if you don't have a specific person in mind. Even if there is someone you've set your sights on, you would probably benefit from going through this process first. It will give you better insight into your own romantic potential, and you just might meet someone else you like even more . . . you never know.

The first step is a visit to your Cosmic Candy Store, designed to help you align your personal magnetism and your romantic magic so that you can ultimately find the best partner for you. Some of you will be so enchanted by the process of attraction that you may linger here for a while. After all, you may have a sweet tooth that demands variety.

The Cosmic Candy Store is where you go to sample various romantic prospects. You may find that some of these treats don't tickle your palate, but you may also find that you really enjoy a chocolate truffle more than the usual cherry drops. You'll never know until you try, and these spells will get you started on the right track.

The second category of spells for attraction is used in attracting a specific individual you have found in the Cosmic Candy Store. You may think that once you've met this person, your work is done. It just may be, but in the event that you need to keep the tender first flame of attraction going, these spells are designed to build that spark into a firm, ongoing fire.

✦

Step one: creating the Cosmic Candy Store

♥

These spells are for attracting people who have the *potential* for becoming your lover. Some of these people may not be right for a long-term relationship or for commitment, and you may not choose to pursue a romantic relationship with each one of them. You might have to try a few bonbons that don't agree with you just so you know what they taste like. These spells should, if used correctly, present you with a Cosmic Candy Store filled with tempting options. You can make your own choices once the variety of the shop is presented to you. But don't rush into a five-pound bag of anything until you've sampled a few ounces of the sweets you've attracted.

Why you need the Cosmic Candy Store

If you are looking for a committed relationship, you may think this is only a baby step toward what you want. In reality, sampling and selecting is a necessary skill for you to learn, so that you can cast your net far and wide into the sea of prospective mates. These spells increase your choices, and knowing your choices makes you a better judge of what is best for you.

We have been led to believe that finding love is like playing musical chairs, that if you don't hurry up and find your mate, you'll be left standing alone. This is absolutely not true. Unhappy unions often result when commitment is made out of fear of loneliness rather than out of love for the other person. The practices of attraction enable you to play around with your possibilities and eventually follow through with a relationship that is really right for you.

The Cosmic Candy Store is also good for the times in your life when a committed relationship isn't appropriate but you'd like a little romance. For people putting a great deal of energy into work concerns, for those dealing with health issues, and for people still healing from the end of a long-term relationship, these spells for attraction are quite useful.

You've heard of rebound relationships, in which a rejected lover finds someone to fill the void, and encounters another relationship that is often doomed to finish unpleasantly. The Cosmic Candy Store can keep you in the flow of romantic life without making you feel that you need to seal yourself into a relationship before the time is right. A little light romance may keep you distracted from your troubles.

Sometimes you just don't have time for a relationship due to work or a duty of some sort. Sometimes you need a little something to color your daily grind, to add spark to your life, and to remind you that you are an attractive person.

These spells are also useful for what I call "practice dating," when you've been out of circulation for a while, for whatever reason, and you want to start in on the social scene again but are a little reticent about the dating game. It is okay to be cautious, but there is no reason to believe that dating again will be dismal, uncomfortable, and unfulfilling. There are plenty of people out there who are just like you—normal, decent people looking for good times and pleasant company. You must shake off whatever myths you may harbor about how difficult it is to date, or how unpleasant the experience can be, so that you can take advantage of some lighthearted fun.

The Candy Store mind-set

You don't need to *learn* how to be attractive—you already have what it takes. The Candy Store mindset starts with taking stock of your assets and "owning" them, which means admitting to yourself that you have attractive qualities and taking pride in them. Spells for attraction start with the way you see yourself; if you see yourself as unappealing, or weak in some way, your spell will carry that with it. Just to be sure you're clear on this, take an inventory.

Your ability to attract is directly related to your own feelings about yourself. If *you* have trouble identifying what is attractive about you, you can be sure that other people will have similar trouble. If you know what is attractive, so will they.

The physical you

Perhaps people are always telling you how beautiful your eyes are, or how lovely your hair is, or what a beautiful voice you have. Take a look at your physical self, and claim and honor your strengths. If you feel that your ankles are especially pretty, that is an asset. If your brow is attractive, congratulate yourself on this beauty. The point here is to see what you feel proud of, what you like to show off. Being humble here will get you nowhere. And don't let media standards get in the way of what you perceive as beauty. You do not have to look like a waif or a muscle man to be attractive. It works for some of us, but not for others. This is the great flexibility of beauty. It truly *is* in the eye of the beholder, and what you're working on here is attracting appropriate beholders of your beauty.

Your inner beauty

Your attractiveness isn't just physical, either. The adage that "love is blind" comes from an old truth that your inner spirit is your center of attractiveness. When inner spirits connect, love often results.

Think of the so-called beautiful people you've met who aren't really so attractive. Recall people you've been attracted to without an obvious physical connection. This experience supports the idea that attractiveness and attraction is more "magic and musk" than looks and smiles.

In order to understand your inner beauty, pay attention to how you react to new people in your life. Are you shy? Are you judgmental or critical? When you meet someone for the first time, do you tend to like or dislike that person right away? Assessing your reactions to people you meet, whether they are romantic interests or not, will help you learn about your emotional generosity and how open you are to new people.

The more you are able to listen to what people have to say, and to allow yourself to form an opinion slowly, the more openly they will perceive you. If you can relax and show people a little bit about yourself while allowing them to do the same, you will find it very easy to attract romantic prospects. If you are very closed, you will need to work hard on this part of yourself in order to get the attraction spells to work.

Beware of self-sabotage

You may think you have all the assets and openness it takes to cast a strong attraction spell, but there is one more step in evaluating yourself. This is the problem of self-sabotage, which is "unselling" yourself by pointing out a weakness in the guise of honesty. If you go into a candy store and complain about your weight, you'll have everyone wondering what you're doing there.

Shelly was a pretty woman in her mid-forties, just coming out of a divorce. She wanted to start meeting new men; in her single days, years before, she hadn't found this hard to do. Her mind-set about dating was healthy and somewhat optimistic. People always remarked on the loveliness of her smile and her reddish-brown hair. Her sense of attractiveness was pretty good, or so she thought.

Shelly began to date a man a few years younger whom she met through the gym to which they both belonged. After a few rounds in the weight room, they agreed to go for coffee. A few dates later, Shelly and her beau were having an ice cream cone after seeing a movie. The movie had been a romantic comedy in which the heroine was beautiful, thin, tall, young, and just about perfect in every way. As they were discussing these admirable physical qualities, Shelly grew afraid that her own body wasn't good enough, that she wasn't attractive enough for this guy. She started expressing her insecurities about her body at length. Since they'd met in a health club, she also explained her workout strategy. When the date ended, he didn't call her again.

Shelly complained to a girlfriend about how surprised she was that he hadn't called. But, after hearing the details of their last date, her friend wasn't. She pointed out that since Shelly had made her self-described physical shortcomings into a commercial for her own unattractiveness, it wasn't so strange that he hadn't called again. Shelly drew attention to qualities he may never have noticed. It certainly wasn't necessary to go on about how much work her body needed.

It makes no sense to seize upon your own insecurity and serve it up to a romantic prospect. If you think you have a flaw, keep your opinion to yourself and do not point it out. Often other people do not see flaws where you do, unless you ask them to. In this chapter, you will also find useful spells for casting a glamour (see page 75).

Shelly's example may seem extreme, but there are many subtle ways to sabotage yourself when you are attracting potential lovers. Low self-esteem and insecurity can make it hard for you to allow people to be attracted to you. Shyness can keep people from approaching you, because quiet people can look aloof, snobbish, or uninterested. Pushiness can be equally harmful, as can the need to take control of the situation. Bossy people create a distance between themselves and others by always needing to have the last word.

You may not even know that you have self-sabotaging problems until you find that your attraction spells aren't working well. Self-sabotaging behavior is a result of being in a stressful, risky situation, and you unconsciously reduce the risk by keeping people away from you. Pay attention to how you react to new prospects and see if you lapse into a behavior that keeps things from progressing. Here's a sampler of patterns of sabotage:

Being too critical of a prospect

Choosing the same "type" over and over

Expecting too much

Not expecting enough

Losing your self-respect

Giving too much while not being able to receive

The essential art of play

Our Western work ethic, combined with the emphasis on rational thought, has bludgeoned us into thinking that playfulness is frivolous and even guilt-inducing behavior. It is a sad comment on our culture that so many of us feel that having a good time and enjoying ourselves is a luxury that must be defended.

The art of play is one of the most important ingredients for romance and attraction. Playfulness is *not* just for kids. Adults need to be playful too. We usually express this with our devotion to sports, comedy, or entertainment, but romantic playfulness seems to be a lost art. Somehow, the serious side of life has taken many of us away from the natural pleasures of play, and left us thinking life has to be a real grind. With many voices in the media reporting pressing issues of our times—including crime, war, drug abuse, and the constant coverage of people doing bad things to each other—it is no wonder that we forget that the lighter side of life even exists. Never fear, though; it is exceedingly easy to learn to play again.

Flirtation

There are many ways to play with attraction and romance. Flirtation is the first place to start. Flirting is a very important part of the attraction process, and it is a lot of fun. For some, flirting is second nature, while for others, it is the most painful and difficult social skill they have to learn.

The art of flirtation is not grounded in a rational process; it is entirely playful. Humor is always an excellent asset for flirtation, although innuendo and suggestiveness also work. You need to find your own flirtation mode, and you can shift it according to your mood.

Leigh, a professor of philosophy, is a basically shy woman in public, but a strong and assertive individual with people she knows well. She had never considered herself a flirt, since she had been entrenched in the academic world her whole life. She looked at me with fear when I started to lecture her about flirtation. She claimed that she didn't have a clue about how to flirt, but she had had several serious relationships in her past, so I knew this couldn't be true, since all romantic relationships start with some sort of flirtation "dance."

Leigh thought there was no way she could ever be as winning and charming as the other women she saw around her. It took one spell and one night out with a group of friends to rid her of that impression. Unlike her usual quiet dinners, this group spontaneously decided to go to a nightclub. Leigh had done her flirtation spell before going out, thinking that she could practice in the safety of her friends' company. She was highly amused to find herself chatting with a man at the bar and dancing with him for a while. When he asked for her phone number, Leigh had a fear reaction and left the club to go back home on her own. Nevertheless, she now boasts proudly about her ability to flirt, and I think she has a lot more fun, too.

Flirtation can also help lift your energy so that you are more approachable. As a general rule, it is easier to attract people when you are not carrying around a two-ton weight of expectancy. You will be more approachable if you remind yourself that this is just a light-hearted game of hanging out your hankie to see who wants to catch it. Don't be afraid if someone you don't want to flirt with stops by for a chat. Just because someone chats with you does not mean you have to marry that person. So lighten up! Playfulness keeps your life interesting, and can help a great deal when you need a break from the serious side of life.

Janine tried a spell for attraction when she was transferred to Houston from Chicago. She didn't want to start a relationship with anyone until she got her bearings, but she didn't want to stay home all the time, either. She was invited to a party by some friends, and cast her simple spell before going, concentrating on a lighthearted, playful evening. She found the warm, chivalrous attitudes of Houston men a refreshing change from the more practical men of her Chicago past, and she loved it. She flirted her head off, thinking of herself as a sort of Scarlett O'Hara, and gave her business cards out to several prospective admirers. She didn't have time to think too hard about what she was doing, because she got swept into the spirit of the game of playfulness and flirtation. She realized afterward that the spell had done its work. She was most proud to find that she could flirt with the best of those Southern girls, and that she could be a real coquette when she wanted to be. Janine had learned to play and be played with, in a most invigorating game of flirtation.

Personal atmosphere

Playing also requires a certain attitude, what I call a "personal atmosphere." You need to emit an energy that entices the people around you to play with you. If you have this energy going for you, then you are unlikely ever to hear those dreaded words "lighten up."

Tim, a lawyer at a high-powered firm in Pittsburgh, walked around with a heavy atmosphere that made women think he was a drag. His intense working hours kept him from having a strong social life. His dismay about not having enough free time intruded upon the free time he *did* have, and made him seem depressed. He was always complaining when he wasn't working. Tim did a spell for attraction out of curiosity, since his female friends were telling him that he needed to change his attitude. He went to a baseball game with friends, and sat next to a stranger in the bleachers who was a rootin'-tootin' fan around his age. She had Tim yelling and doing the wave just by the force of her enthusiasm, which had also knocked a soda out of his hand. She bought him a soda, he bought her popcorn, they exchanged cards, and he dated her a few times. He had been caught off guard and had forgotten his woes long enough to meet someone just for the fun of it. He has since loosened up a bit, and he still does his attraction spell whenever there is an opportunity. He likes to play, now that he knows how to.

Personal atmosphere also sends messages about what you are looking for. Linda thought that her beauty and height kept men from approaching her. Her blond hair, green eyes, and five-foot-eight frame seemed to mark her as a model type, unapproachable because she was so attractive. Linda's male friends laughed at this, telling her that her looks were an asset, not a liability. They also told her that they thought her attitude seemed more appropriate to husband-shopping than to just having a relaxed good time.

Linda did a spell for attraction and concentrated on lightening up her atmosphere. The spell worked. She opened up her opportunities to meet men who might or might not be relationship possibilities. She was surprised to find herself more talkative and having more fun. Of course, she met more men. Her personal energy shifted to allow someone in. It didn't take long for her to start practice-dating. A year later she was ready for her spell for commitment.

Practice-dating

Not only do we not know much about play, but many of us don't know how to date anymore. Just the idea of dating can cause the burliest of men to break out in a sweat, and the most confident woman to lose her confidence. Entire talk shows are devoted to the subject of dating, as are feature articles in women's magazines every month. Dating is hard to start, but once you've overcome your fear of it, you'll begin to enjoy it.

Practice-dating allows you to set up a less threatening situation. All you have to do is get yourself a date with *anyone*. He or she does not have to be someone you expect to continue seeing. Just go out and have a good time. The point is to take the pressure off of the experience. With the spells for attraction, you should be able to create all sorts of possibilities to enjoy the company of another person, even if that person is not appropriate for a relationship.

It is perfectly honorable and a normal course of social interaction to practice-date, and if you are asked out, it is perfectly okay to accept, even if you don't think the person who asked you is right for you. You are also encouraged to ask people for dates. It's really easy to ask someone to go to a movie or to dinner if you don't have a lot of ego invested in his or her response. After all, it's only for practice. I happen to think of all my first dates this way, and it takes the edge off my fear.

Practice-dating is also a good playground for experimentation. You can cast atmospheric spells, energetic spells, and spells for a glamour to see how they feel. You can cast a spell to control the atmosphere so that you don't get put into an awkward position. Just be sure not to cast a romantic spell until you know you want a romantic encounter.

$\mathcal{S}$tep two: going for the one you want

♥

If you have found a person you want to attract, and you want to try to establish a relationship, you can focus your energy on a specific spell to help make this happen. You are urged to read this section carefully, because these spells are woven delicately, and your energy must be well aligned—meaning that you must have clarity within yourself. This clarity will help ensure a powerful spell that won't bring on unnecessary side effects.

To pull in the energy between you and another person, your spells need to be clear of any of your own emotional stickiness. It is important to remember that whatever you put out, you get back, and if you are trying to control another person, you will probably end up being controlled yourself.

Checklist for personal clarity

1. Before you cast this spell, have you actually met this person?

If you haven't, go back to the Cosmic Candy Store. These spells are only for people you are personally exposed to, and who you feel could be a good match for you. (No fantasies here.)

2. Is this person free to date you?

Don't try these spells on someone who is already attached to someone else. *You are bound to get burned.*

3. Do you have any hidden feelings about why you want this person?

If you want to attract a particular person to prove something, you probably won't have the kind of success you want. Also, if you are toying with someone's affections without regard for how he or she might feel, you are setting yourself up for getting hurt, not to mention hurting the other person.

4. Are you using this person to get over someone else?

Not only will this spell not help with mending a broken heart, but it will probably make you feel worse. Cast your spells for healing your heart and visit the Candy Store before you get into attractions.

If you can get through the questions above without lying to yourself, you are ready to begin the process of attracting the one you want. This type of magic can be likened to the way the spider weaves its invisible web to catch its prey. However, the analogy stops there. This is not an exercise in devouring your romantic prospect; you just want him or her to stop by long enough for love to begin weaving your courses together.

You weave your web by creating opportunities for you to be together. This spell isn't for wishful thinking or fantasizing about romantic trysts; it is a more practical application of magic in order to bring about situations where you can see each other. It may be at a seminar or a party, or at the bakery—it doesn't matter where, it simply matters that your paths do cross.

Victoria met Ryan at a party last year, and although she felt attracted to him and he expressed interest in her, she knew that he had a girlfriend and didn't encourage him. She didn't see him again, although she later heard through friends that he had broken up with his girlfriend. Ten months later she ran into him at another party. Victoria was friendly, but he seemed to want to avoid talking to her, which baffled her, since she still felt chemistry between them. He seemed uncomfortable, and Victoria felt it was just embarrassment.

Victoria, an adventurous type, cast a spell to open up the opportunities for them to meet again and, if possible, to pursue some romantic path. Her spell to bring them together under more social circumstances materialized in their chance meetings at a Super Bowl party, on the street in front of a friend's house, and in line at a movie. The line at the movie was particularly good, she thought, since Victoria was with a date and Ryan was by himself. It seemed to take the pressure off seeing him. It also seemed to do the trick. Ryan called her for a date shortly afterward, and they still see each other.

The spell Victoria cast focused on opening up opportunities to meet Ryan in natural settings, so that they would have the chance to make something happen. This spell is a safe one in the realm of attraction spells, since it doesn't directly affect the other person.

Amy, a sales executive, chanced a more dramatic spell, after her constant flirtation with her coworker, Danny, got her no more than an occasional lunch. She decided that she had to get him out of the office situation and outside of a workday to find out if there could be anything between them, so she cast a spell to create a romantic opportunity. She knew that this could be a risky spell, because it could throw off their friendship, or worse, she could feel rejected.

Her spell took some time to manifest, but, when a sudden snow-storm closed their offices, she found herself getting a lift back to her apartment from Danny. She offered to give him dinner in return, and to her surprise, he accepted. In the warmth of her home, they relaxed and got to know each other more. Danny confessed that he had a long-distance girlfriend whom he was thinking of marrying, which dampened Amy's flame considerably. While the music, the weather, and the mood conspired to encourage romance, Amy let her wishes go when she heard this news. She had no interest in getting into a dead-end affair.

Once you've got a good handle on the fact that your chosen person is both romantically available and interested in you, you can add to the spells for opportunity by increasing your attractiveness to that person.

In casting these spells, which are similar to commitment spells, you need to be very clear with your motives. It is not wise to cast these spells if you are already lusting for marriage at this early stage. That outcome is not appropriate until you've gotten to the stage of verbalizing your love for the other person. These spells help you get to the "I love you" point, if that is to be achieved, but you must allow it to happen in its own time; you cannot force someone to love you.

Pushing yourself onto someone else against their own will is akin to spiritual rape, and you will most certainly find yourself paying a heavy price for it because you have interfered with free will. It may be useful to remember that when or if you are tempted to take matters into your own hands, you could be missing the true love of your life, the one who is absolutely perfect and who loves you as much as you desire. Real love, the kind you're looking for, does not need too much encouragement to manifest. So resist casting forceful spells around the one you want; just let the magic take you where you're meant to go.

Follow the spells for your personal attractiveness carefully and be sure to release any willfulness before you cast your spell.

spell basics

♥

There are some common elements for all spells to increase attractiveness. Not all of these elements are used in the spells that follow, but if you have a desire to use them, please do so.

COLORS: Pink to dark pink (not red unless you just want sex)

FLOWERS: Rose, gardenia, jasmine, violet

HERBS: Lavender, orange peel

CRYSTALS: Jade, lapis lazuli, malachite, rose quartz

DAY TO ATTRACT MEN: Friday

DAY TO ATTRACT WOMEN: Tuesday

TIME OF THE DAY: Third hour of darkness

TIME OF THE MONTH: Between the new Moon and the full Moon

primary spell for
ATTRACTING ROMANTIC
PROSPECTS, PART I

On a Thursday during a waxing Moon,
in the first hour after sunset:

Light a purple candle and place it before a bowl of water.
Hold a mirror up to the candle, the water, and then to your face.
Gaze into your own eyes.

Concentrate on your beauty,
your lovability, your desirability.

Hold the mirror up to the candle again.

SAY ALOUD:
In the grace of the Universe
and in the abundance of love,
I affirm I am greatly desirable
and open to the bounty of love around me.
The flow of love, romance, and partnership is ever abundant,
and in line with the greater good, I create and attract romance.

With your fingertips, put water on the
top of your head, in your mouth, and on your heart center.

Blow out the candles.

primary spell for
ATTRACTING ROMANTIC
PROSPECTS, PART II

On a Friday during a waxing Moon,
in the third hour of darkness:

Offer pink roses in a vase with water to Venus,
the Goddess of Love.

In a bowl made of natural materials, place:
4 pinches of fresh lavender
a piece of red apple with the skin
4 drops of water

Light a pink candle.

SAY ALOUD:
I am open to love, I attract love,
I provide love
in my life and for the greater good.
Venus brings me love
for playfulness, delight, and joy.

Take a bite of the apple.

Burn or dispose of the offering during the ensuing full Moon.

spell for
INCREASING PERSONAL MAGNETISM

to attract men
On a Friday evening during a waxing Moon:

Blend oils or perfumes of the scents that appeal to you.
Choose from
rose
lavender
jasmine
musk
ylang-ylang

to attract women
On Tuesday during a waxing Moon:

Blend the oils that appeal to you.
Choose from
musk
patchouly
cinnamon
carnation
vanilla

Before going out,
bathe with rosebuds and lovage.

When you enter social situations,
wear a drop of your oil blend on your heart center
and wherever else it pleases you.

spell for

CASTING A GLAMOUR AND
DIMINISHING DISCOMFORT

(Do this spell before you enter a social situation,
regardless of the Moon Phase.)

Sit quietly in a room lit
only by the light of a white candle.

Close your eyes.
Feel your own energy.
Notice whether you feel at all uncomfortable.

Breathe deeply, relaxing your energy with a sigh.
With each inhalation, gather glittering energy:
pink, orange, and red colors dance around you.

Whatever insecurity or discomfort you feel,
breathe deeply, relaxing your hold on the discomfort.
Breathe in soft white light.
Feel your energy lighten.
Visualize yourself as you would like to be seen.

Seal the energy of your visualization,
wrapping this vision around you like a cloak.
When you feel secure with this energy,
blow out the candle.

spell for
CREATING A SPACIOUS PERSONAL ATMOSPHERE

(Cast this spell when your mood feels heavy or social situations feel
oppressive. It can be cast in any Moon phase.)

Before going into a social situation,
light a pink or white candle and place a piece of
lapis lazuli in front of you.
Close your eyes.

Release whatever thoughts, reservations, or
fears you may have. Feel your body relaxing.
For the moment, only you matter.

Breathe deeply, visualize a starlit sky.
Breathe in the stars.
Float with the stars.
Be the stars.

When you feel ready, come back to your body
and blow the candle out.

Carry the piece of lapis lazuli with you to
keep your energy in harmony with the lightness
and beauty of the heavens.

spell for attracting the one you want:
CREATING OPPORTUNITIES
TO MEET

On a Friday under a waxing Moon,
in the third hour of darkness:

Make a sachet of
red rose petals
catnip
orange peel

Place the charm before a red candle and a glass of water.

SAY ALOUD:
I enchant this charm to bring

———

to me to investigate the possibility of
a delightful romantic partnership.
I ask this within the greater good.
I affirm I create a mutually beneficial
relationship with respect and spaciousness for us both.
With the blessing of Venus, myself, and
the Universe, I ask that this be done.
So be it.
And so it is.

Blow out the candle.

Carry the sachet with you.

spell for attracting the one you want:
ENCHANTING
A ROMANTIC SETTING

(This spell is to be done on the day the setting is to be used.
Ideally, the space will not be disturbed by anyone other than you or your
intended lover after you cast the atmosphere. Add a vase of
flowers of pink or red color to the setting.)

Before your intended lover arrives,
sit quietly before a lighted pink candle.
Close your eyes and breathe deeply,
relaxing your body and your face in doing so.

Focus on your heart center.
Visualize light coming out of it, emanating from you.
Change the colors of the light from
red to yellow to orange, green, blue, purple, white, and pink.
Stay with the color or colors that are easiest for you.
Fill the room with your light. Breathe your light in and out.

SAY ALOUD:
I enchant this space to support and hold delight, playfulness,
and easy affection. I fill this room with the electric
possibilities of love and light and joyful connection,
for the greater good.
So be it.
And so it is.

Leave the candle burning.

FOUR

SPELLS
FOR
COMMITMENT

You have found love in someone, and you want to make sure that you have a lasting relationship; perhaps you have a commitment from your lover but you want marriage. Commitment also needs staying power. These spells can help bind your relationship with strong, pure, life-enhancing energy.

Spells for commitment: creating it and keeping it
♥

Spells for commitment are of two kinds. The first kind is cast when you want to create a commitment from your lover. This applies when you've met someone and established some kind of binding relationship, but you want a commitment, an understanding that you are together as a couple.

The second kind is cast when you're in a relationship and you are having a hard time with it. These are spells for staying power; they should be used when you feel that your relationship has run aground or is at some kind of plateau, and you need some encouragement to stay within its framework. You may be thinking of straying a bit, or you may just think that the grass is greener on the single side of life. Before you jeopardize your commitment by an action that may cause serious damage, try these spells.

A caveat
♥

Spells for creating commitment carry with them a tremendous responsibility. You need to be very clear about your feelings, and you must be sensitive to your own desire to control your lover's actions. These spells bind you to someone with all that exists now. If there is hostility, it will follow you. If there is fear, it won't be allayed just by obtaining a commitment.

Additionally, this is a spell through which you are imposing your wishes on another individual. If you put your will before the welfare of others, it is black magic. To add safety to your spell, make sure you always ask that it be done for the greater good and within the free will of all. Believe me, you wouldn't want the commitment any other way.

Beyond the responsibility of initiating commitment, you may also find that the spell reacts within you as an individual. Your personal issues about intimate relationships will come up and must be addressed within the creation of your commitment. You can be sure that if you don't work these issues out, you'll run into problems in your relationship.

It may help you to remember that your partner serves as a mirror for you. If you find that your lover is having commitment problems, look within yourself and you may find your own issues that need to be resolved.

Commitment spells: not necessarily marriage
♥

These spells will help you create more stable energy in your partnership while maintaining the passion and delight you now have.

As with all spells, you must allow the magic of the universe to guide you, so that the greater good is served for both you and your lover. If you find that these spells don't take hold within a three-to-six-month time frame, it may be that you have the wrong partner, or that you have spun a spell too early in your relationship. In magic, marriage is not the legal contract, so you may already have the permanence you desire, and just lack society's trappings. It may not be possible to cement your relationship legally, but this does not mean your love is not committed for the long term.

Spell preparation for creating commitment
♥

When you cast this spell, pay attention to how you feel about the long term. Do you want a guarantee that you'll have a lifetime commitment? Is the long term for you just a year or two? Realize how flexible or inflexible you are. If you can allow the magic to take you to the best possible place in time, your spell will be most powerful. This means letting go of your own timetable. After all, you're involving another person here, and even though you think you may know what is best for him or her, you don't.

How about fear? Are you willing to take the chance that your spell won't work? If you are casting this spell out of fear that your relationship is ending, and you don't want it to, you may be putting a lot of your will into the spell, rather than your intention. As noted in chapter 1, willfulness isn't conducive to successful spell casting. Try to identify your fear, if you have any, and breathe space around it so that you can create a strong spell. Fear weakens magic.

Harriet and Jordan dated for five years. He wanted to marry her; she wasn't ready. Jordan, a strong skeptic, was persuaded by a pal to seek the help of a popular local spell maker, who worked in the back room of a botanica. Although Jordan didn't believe in it, he went along out of curiosity. In answering questions from the spell maker about his emotional commitment to Harriet, it became clear to him that he was marrying her to avoid being single. He expressed concern for his friends who didn't have anyone in their lives, and he acknowledged that he was scared of AIDS and felt that it was safer to be married. Jordan loved Harriet, but he hadn't really considered the consequences: marriage is for good. The spell maker got him thinking about the permanence of his desire for commitment, and he saw that he wasn't really doing it for the right reasons. Jordan and Harriet are still dating, but have no plans for marriage.

Casting a spell may bring up deeper issues around your feelings and your relationship. It is advisable to recognize these issues and work with them so that your commitment is strong and clear.

Before casting the spell, take a good look at your partner. Does this person increase your quality of life? Do you feel that your relationship has somehow brought out good things in you? Although you cannot answer for your partner, do you feel you now contribute to his or her well-being? If so, your relationship will probably take to this spell easily. When relationships are out of balance, spells of commitment can cement them that way, and you could be stuck with a mate that you are continually giving to or taking from, always striving to find the equilibrium.

Shirley had been living with Chuck for a year, but things weren't progressing the way she had hoped. He seemed to have settled into a routine and didn't see the need for marriage. The spark started to fizzle for Shirley. She wanted to relive the days when they had been newly in love, when all Chuck would talk about was marriage. At that time, it had been her idea to wait. She reflected on that, wondering why she hadn't jumped at the opportunity to get engaged when it was offered.

Shirley's spell casting brought out an unexpected reaction: she began to feel sad. She realized that what she really wanted back was the passion in their relationship—the way it was in the early days. She worked with this feeling, and instead of casting the spell for commitment, she turned to the spells for reigniting passion. These spells heated up their passion, and when she felt the relationship was back on track, she cast her spell for commitment. It took four months to work, but on her birthday Chuck presented her with a ring.

Not only is it extremely important that you have a clear understanding of your role in your relationship, but it is also a good idea to have some sense of what you are looking for in the future.

Desiree and Jonathan met at a party and, in the bloom of early love, decided to live together. They found compatibility and friendship as they stayed together, and Jonathan decided that marriage was right for them. They had never discussed children, but Jonathan brought it up casually one day. He was surprised that Desiree had no interest in having children, but supposed it was because she was just too young to care; both of them were in their early twenties. Desiree also thought that marriage was silly if they weren't going to have children, but Jonathan worked at persuading her, and with the help of some spells, Desiree agreed to marriage. Their union was happy until a few years later, when Jonathan wanted to have children. Desiree hadn't changed her mind, and she felt betrayed that he hadn't believed her when she said she wasn't interested in having any. They went to counseling and tried to work it out, but neither could give in. Sadly, they split up.

Because Jonathan hadn't taken her at her word, their marriage was not built on a firm foundation. His belief that she would change colored his thinking and this illusion entered into their union, only to emerge later.

Whatever habits or patterns are set up in your relationship, they will be hard to change once you're in a committed stage. It doesn't mean that you cannot change your own rhythm or your pattern as a couple, and some of the spells in this book are sure to help, but it will take a lot of effort and luck to change the other person, especially if he or she doesn't want to be changed.

When relationships are taken for granted, it is not a good time to make a commitment. Before casting a spell for commitment, take a tally of how much appreciation there is for your love.

◆

Personal integrity checklist for spells for creating commitment

Answer these questions honestly, and you will know if a spell is appropriate.

1. Do you have a time frame in mind, and can you let go of it so that your magic can create the strongest love cycle?

2. Are you casting this spell out of fear that your partner will leave you?

3. Is your willfulness taking over your intention? Do you need this commitment?

4. Are you really just tired or afraid of being alone?

5. Can you see your partner clearly, or are you only seeing what you want him or her to be?

If you find that some of these questions arouse fears or ambiguous answers, look at what is causing that reaction and try to identify your motives. If you find that your motivation for commitment is not in line with what has been described here, or that your love has conditions to it, you may not have the success you desire. In the worst case, you could create a commitment that someday you will need to break or re-form.

If you find yourself open to the possibilities of your relationship, you will probably have success with this spell. If your intention is clear, you have love and the blessing of love returned, and you have trust that whatever happens, it can be so.

Spells for staying power

♥

Scott and Lanie had been going out for three years, and their families wanted them to marry. Although they were in love and had already anticipated getting married, Scott was unsettled and felt that he hadn't experienced life enough. Lanie felt his discontent and wondered if he was simply taking her for granted. He said he needed to spend more time on his own, even play the field, before he got married. Lanie was very wise. She let him go, using a spell that created space between her and Scott, instead of breaking up with him, as was her first impulse. She also knew that trapping him into marriage was not a good idea. She didn't want him to feel that he was missing something.

Scott and Lanie told their families that they were having a trial separation for three months. Lanie found that it was tolerable, being on her own, flirting and going out with her girlfriends without Scott. She missed him, though, and of course he missed her. Scott needed his time alone, but he also realized how much he relied on Lanie for companionship. His few dates with other women were nowhere near as fulfilling as his time with her. After six weeks they got back together, and soon became engaged.

Lanie used her spaciousness spell to make it easier on her while Scott had his time alone. Scott's time alone showed him how deeply he loved Lanie. Creating spaciousness can be the most compelling spell for commitment in cases like this.

Sometimes love relationships go through periods of stagnancy, inertia, or boredom that are not just related to sexual passions. You may think that you've run out of steam, or that your relationship has run its course. It might be so, but most probably you're experiencing a trial in staying power. Since we live in a society that expects immediate gratification, you may think that things have to get better fast or they won't get better at all. What you need at times like this is tolerance and spaciousness for your relationship to grow in its own time.

Tolerance is practically demanded in all love relationships. When you're gritting your teeth at the most annoying habit your lover has, when your mate is acting like the Geek from Hell, you are in need of tolerance to get you through it.

Sandy and Rich had been married for four years when Sandy decided to start an herb garden in their tiny backyard. She dug up the ground, bought books on herb gardens, obsessed about fertilizer, weeds, and the types of herbs she should plant. Rich thought the hobby was good for her, until she expanded her plans and decided to build a greenhouse. He knew things were getting out of hand when Sandy talked about traveling to see certain herbaceous borders she'd been reading about in her new magazines. He thought that she was getting a little obsessive, not to mention very dull. They began to fight about the time and money being spent on Sandy's new hobby, and the lack of time they were spending together. Rich consulted Sandy's best friend one day, although he felt a little disloyal in doing so. He received the confirmation that Sandy was going through a very trying phase, and, unexpectedly, he got information about a spell for tolerance to help him get through it. His spell helped him ease up on his desire to control Sandy's attention, and gave him back his sense of humor. He teased her about having dill instead of children. She ignored him and carried on with her efforts, but eventually she took a part-time job at a commercial greenhouse nearby. This satisfied her need to garden and allowed her to have a life with Rich again. His spell for tolerance helped him to see the humor and "lighten up" during Sandy's obsessive period.

Sometimes tolerance in a broader form is needed, as when your lover is being selfish or jealous. The trick of tolerance is the ability to rise above the immediate situation, to shift your ego out of the way long enough for you to see how unimportant control is. Tolerance allows you to coexist with the person you love, even when you can't feel that love all the time.

These spells will not work, however, if your lover is being abusive or unkind. Behavior that hurts you or is unhealthy for you in any way won't be supported by a spell, since it is not compatible with the greater good. If you are experiencing cruelty or abuse in any form, please see chapter 7 for spells on severing ties.

Useful tips for enhancing spells for commitment
♥

For spells of commitment, you will benefit by having a picture of your beloved with you. Also, if you possess some token of love, given to you in an intimate moment, your spell energy will be more powerful. As you may have imagined, your lover's hair, nail clippings (if you can stand it), or an article of clothing will also contribute energy. These are highly personal, and hence highly charged, representations of your lover. With spells of commitment, you are basically conjuring your lover's energy along with your own; therefore, the more you have of his or her essence, the better.

You may use these personal items to accompany you in your Primary Spell, and you can use these and other ingredients in the other spells you cast. Music you both enjoy is powerful, and you are encouraged to sing along while you are preparing or casting your spell. The power of voice greatly enhances the magic.

Wear a fragrance your lover likes, or burn a favorite incense. In a way, you are creating the perfect romantic and compatible atmosphere. It is in the safety of this energy that you can release your magic in its most powerful essence.

spell basics

♥

COLORS: Green and red

FLOWERS: Red and pink roses

HERBS: Lavender, lovage

CRYSTAL: Diamond

DAY OF THE WEEK: Friday

TIME OF THE DAY: Third hour of darkness

TIME OF THE MONTH: Before a full Moon

primary spell
FOR COMMITMENT

On a Friday during the third hour of darkness:

Light a red candle and a white candle.
Place a crystal glass of water in front of you.
If you have a diamond, any size or quality, hold it in your hand.
Gather your energy so that you are still.
Breathe deeply, sighing aloud in your exhalation.
Visualize your loved one, see that person in your mind's eye,
touch him or her with your imagination, feel your love.

Breathe your love through your heart.
Feel the energy of your relationship in your love.

SAY ALOUD:
I ask that this love be protected and allowed to flourish.
I ask that both _____ and I grow
together in mind, in heart, and in spirit.
I affirm our permanent union is blessed for us
and for the greater good.
So be it.
And so it is.

Slowly raise your hands in front of you
to signify that you cast the spell into the Universe.
Sip the water and blow out the flame.

spell for a
LONG AND HAPPY
RELATIONSHIP

On a Friday during the third hour of darkness:

Light three candles: deep red, purple, and white.

SAY ALOUD:
I ask the Goddess Branwen to bestow
true love on my union with _____.

Breathe your love into your heart.
Place a potted cyclamen in the bedroom, and water the plant.
Place a red apple in front of the candles.

SAY ALOUD:
I ask that this be done for the greater good.
So be it.
And so it is.

Gaze at the flames in each candle,
and when you are ready,
blow them out.

spells to create
PERMANENCE
IN THE ATMOSPHERE

During the first hour of darkness on a Monday:

Put fresh flowers with water in a pink or clear crystal vase.
Choose from
jasmine
violets
red roses
asters

During the fourth hour of darkness on a Sunday:

Create a sachet* using
fresh dill
spearmint
dried orange peel
Dab water on the outside of this charm.
Keep the sachet in the room you use the most together.
Create more sachets for other rooms.

If you have a fickle lover, add caraway to your sachet.

*See Appendix, "Charm Making for Beginners."

more spells for permanence
IN THE ATMOSPHERE

During the second hour of darkness on a Thursday:

Burn incense of
rose, sandalwood, cinnamon, and patchouly
to bring expansion
and abundance to your union.

During the first hour of darkness on a Monday:

Place ferns and pieces of jade in your living space.

When possible, cook for your lover with cumin seeds,
which enhance devotion.*

---

*Although use of love potions is contrary to the laws of white magic, cooking with herbs natural to our diets is acceptable.

charms to give to
YOUR LOVER

Fresh yarrow flowers, which grow
wild from May to October,
keep a couple together for
seven years.
Give fresh yarrow to your lover,
or make a gift of a charm of yarrow.

Slip a sachet of orange blossoms
into your lover's pocket, or
leave them in a discreet place where
he or she lives.

Never give yellow or white roses.

spell for staying power:
SPACIOUSNESS

On a Thursday under a waxing Moon,
in the first hour of darkness:

Light a white candle for your relationship.
Light a blue candle for understanding and tranquillity.
Place small amounts of lavender in each corner of the room.

Place before the candles
dried sage
borage
a carnation
a bowl of water

Remember a time when you and your lover were in
perfect harmony.
Feel this time, take yourself back to it, relive it. Breathe it.

SAY ALOUD:
Our love thrives and grows and remains in our hearts in all
space and all time, in support of the greater good.
So be it.
And so it is.

Blow out the candle, use the water for your plants.

Leave the herbs out, inconspicuously if necessary.

spell for staying power:
TOLERANCE

During a waxing Moon, light a white candle for your relationship.
Light an orange candle for kindness and encouragement.

In a shell or any other natural receptacle, place
bay leaf
dried sage
a small amount of vanilla
water

SAY ALOUD:
I affirm that I am committed to this relationship.
I affirm my love for _____.
Under the power of the Moon,
I ask for clarity and light in my commitment.
I declare my faith in our love,
and I claim my power to protect it.
I hold the greatness of our love with gratitude and respect.
I know this to be true and say
So be it.
And so it is.

Blow out the candles.

At the full Moon, empty the
contents of the receptacle.

FIVE

SPELLS FOR
FERTILITY

Spells for fertility are based on the concept of manifesting the love that you and your partner share. Consciously creating a new life is certainly the most sacred ritual we are able to share with our partners, and its magic is both profound and mysterious.

When is the time to cast a spell for fertility?

♥

You don't have to wait until you have problems with conception to use your fertility spell. There are some very simple approaches that do not require complicated procedures or time. Many women unconsciously create the energy to form a new life. Being more conscious about the process is simply living more fully in the flow of your own energy and in the energy of the Cosmos. The experience of a fully conscious life is much more satisfying. You may find even more pleasure in the process of conception and pregnancy when you understand it on a spiritual level.

The relationship between spells and medical help

♥

Recent scientific advancements have made it possible for couples to have children even when the odds are against them. For some, this poses ethical questions; for others, it gives them the only hope they can cling to when it seems that there is no other way.

The relationship between spells for fertility and scientific method can be complementary; there is no reason why you cannot pursue both paths. However, since spell casting relates to more organic processes, you may want to start here. In the spell experience, you can learn a lot about your body and your life-force pattern as it relates to the childbearing process. This is not to say that you won't learn anything if you are getting medical assistance, but your body may be shifting from its natural rhythm if you are undergoing hormone therapy or some other treatment.

The heart of the matter rests in your hope, faith, and intention that you want to create a new life as a manifestation of the love you share with your partner and/or to share your nurturing and love with a being from your own body. Science or spells aside, these qualities are at the very root of your ultimate success.

Your flow and the Cosmic Flow
♥

The female cycle is akin to the phases of the Moon. The body prepares for an egg just as the new Moon awaits the growing light. As the egg finds a home in the womb, so the Moon grows full. The disappointed egg departs with some blood flow as the Moon fades into the sky, darkening before it is reborn in the new Moon. The obvious difference here is that the Moon doesn't get pregnant or give birth. However, the reason it is important to understand the Moon cycle is to learn about your own cycle.

Many women's menstrual cycles are synchronized with the Moon. My friend Susan, like clockwork, grows into an advanced state of PMS as the Moon reaches its fullest, and knows exactly when to look forward to her period. She recently shifted her vitamin regimen and has considerably decreased her PMS. Nonetheless, the full Moon is her signal that her period is on the way.

Some women are reversed, and tend to ovulate with the full Moon and to shed the flow with the new Moon. Some women don't regulate with the Moon at all. It doesn't matter what rhythm your body chooses, but only that you begin to understand it. Here, science can help you if you have no clue where to begin. You can buy kits to help you identify when you ovulate, so that you can begin to track your own cycle.

Your cycle is your personal flow, an energy cycle that you have created and that is perfect for the needs of your body. This is where some negativity can enter into the picture. There are many women who experience what are termed irregular cycles, and their periods don't follow an obvious pattern; they don't know what to expect, or when. There are drugs to increase regularity, which can be helpful; however, this approach implies that there is something wrong with the way your cycle works, that somehow your body is imperfect in this way.

Spell casting works with the flow of your personal energy, and if that energy is "irregular," that is how it is meant to be. Irregular cycles do not imply infertility. The magic of conception isn't dictated by the frequency of your periods. Doris, for example, was on birth-control pills, the most effective form of birth control (besides abstinence) that exists. The pill prevents ovulation, that crucial release of the egg, so that the sperm can find no place to call home, and also creates a hostile environment so that the egg cannot thrive. Doris was on the pill for ten years, always taking her pill at the same time of day. She missed one pill, one day. She wasn't worried, since she'd heard of many women missing three days at a time and not getting pregnant. Nine months later her daughter was born. Irregular or nonexistent cycles do not mean you won't have a baby.

The most important issue here is how you feel about your body. Try not to allow judgments of how fast you should conceive or how often you should get your period make you doubt yourself. Do not make an adversary of your body. If you have perfect health, you have a perfect body.

In spell casting, conception is a point where your flow coincides with the divine flow of the universe. This is what I call Cosmic Flow. Once you respect the Cosmic Flow you have much more power in your spells.

As with all spells, the Cosmic Flow demands faith and belief from you and your partner. Your spell participation must be integrated with your belief that you are fertile and that, when it is right, you can conceive. Your partner's belief is also required. The responsibility of this creation lies between you.

You can increase your connection to the Cosmic Flow by opening up to the natural flow of our natural world. Garden, grow plants in your house, care for animals, or simply take time to observe the birds or squirrels that live around you. Watch their patterns of life, how they feed, gather, and seek shelter. The natural world offers us a direct connection to the Cosmic Flow.

You don't have to become a naturalist to see that nature has patterns everywhere, and that, somehow, we all coexist as our patterns interweave with others. We who live in industrialized countries are the people who are most disconnected from the Cosmic Flow. We fight it all the time, with our insistence on overriding nature. We use air-conditioning to help control our climate, because we think we have to be productive year-round. Agrarian cultures worked the land, but took siestas when the sun became too hot. We act as though a snowstorm is an enemy plot to keep us from getting to work. Maybe it's just a signal that it's winter, a fallow time when we should be hunkering down instead of getting to work at all costs.

If going with the Cosmic Flow seems a bit radical an idea for you, as it is for many people, you don't have to change your whole life to respect it. Simply notice the patterns of nature and the seasons. This respect and attention will serve to hook you up to the Cosmic Flow.

What about men?

♥

Mysterious as the flow of a woman's cycle can be, the cycle a man goes through is not only mysterious—it is ignored. Men don't have to menstruate to experience changes in libido, energy, or mood. In order to explain irritable or irrational behavior, many women already have concluded that their spouses have some sort of cycle.

I am not going to present a complete model of a man's cycle, but you may find a link in two areas.

First, the more "male" days of the week are Sunday, Tuesday, and Thursday, which are ruled by the Sun, Mars, and Jupiter, respectively. The more feminine, fertile days of Monday and Friday bring out the feminine qualities of the male. These days are good for tenderness and love, and, as mentioned previously, are good days for dating. For men who are concerned with their masculine prowess or virility, the more masculine days are probably a better choice.

The Sun is to men as the Moon is to women, when it comes to cycles. Although the Sun does not pass through phases as the Moon does, it does shift into a different astrological sign every month. Depending on a man's birth sign, the Sun's shift can increase or decrease his energy. When the Sun is in the sign opposite from the birth sign or in the sign three months after, there may be a tense aspect that could interfere with his energy. Also, the full Moon that occurs six months after his birthday can create a tense emotional time.

For instance, an Aries man could be in a less powerful state when the Sun is in Libra, his opposite sign, or in Cancer, the sign three months later than his, after Taurus and Gemini. The full Moon that occurs while the Sun is in Libra is a powerful time for his natural feminine energy to come through, but since it fights the stronger masculine self, this could end up being a tense time.

Further explorations using astrology will reveal much more about a man's personal cycle. You don't have to go that far, though, if you are simply open to the fact that his cycle does exist. Respect for a man's cycle contributes to understanding how and when conception is more or less likely to be achieved.

Dual spell casting
♥

Men are encouraged to participate in fertility spell casting. All spells are significantly stronger when more people are involved. In evoking fertility, the ideal is for both mates to cast the spell. If this is not a likely situation, there are spells for the individual. It will be harder for a man to cast this spell alone than it will be for a woman. Though both sexes are needed for ultimate success, the woman sometimes has a little more control here. Consciously or unconsciously, if the woman does not want to become pregnant, she may be able to override a man's will.

Spell preparation
♥

The question must be asked: Why do you want to have a baby? The answer may be obvious to you, but there are hidden agendas sometimes associated with baby-making.

If you are trying to save your marriage, if you are thinking that having a child will make you feel more whole as a person, if you are having a child to "replace" someone close to you who has died, you could be asking for trouble.

These situations may sound harsh to you. How could someone have a child out of their own need? Unfortunately, it is done all the time. Some women have them for money; some have them because their husbands want them to, or to save a marriage. Some people just have them because it's the thing to do in their family or within their set.

We would not have the population explosion we do if we used more conscious energy in procreation. That is where spells can serve you.

Your spell may work regardless of your hidden agendas, but, in doing the spell, you may identify hidden reasons why you want to create a child. When a child is born for a reason other than simple love and the desire to nurture a new being, at some point you will have to face that reason.

If you feel that you are having a child out of love and the desire to manifest your love, you are already on the right track.

The next step is to evaluate your environment. Do you feel supported and comfortable in your current home and at work? How do you handle pressure? Do you take exercise? Are you obsessive or compulsive about anything, such as weight, food, sex, alcohol, attention? If you can do an honest personal inventory of your emotional comfort level, you will see where there may be pitfalls in your path.

For instance, Robin and her husband decided to start their family. They expected to conceive right away, and when it didn't happen, they got worried. Robin didn't want to go to a fertility expert after only three months of trying, and she discussed her fears with her husband. He didn't think there was anything to worry about, so they kept trying. They both led very busy lives at work, and both had to do a lot of traveling and socializing. They also liked working out. Robin loved to run, and was competing in local races. When she felt pressure, Robin "ran it out," as she put it; running was a way to let off steam. When a friend of hers pointed out that she might have no room in her life for a child, Robin scoffed at her, but the words echoed as days went by. Robin realized that she didn't have a lot of time. She had a very full life and hadn't thought about how this might affect her ability to get pregnant, perhaps in an unconscious way. As Robin became conscious of her own busyness, she realized that she'd have to give some of it up. She decided that running would go first, not the exercise, but the races, the extra miles, the speed work she'd been doing. This left her a new space to see how it felt to be still. She cast a spell at the same time, making a charm for fertility, and placed it next to her bed.

Robin's husband matched her effort to wind down, and stopped running around so much, too. Eventually they spent more time together and, six months later, conceived their first child. They had needed a little stillness to allow their energies to merge together into the Flow, and once they were in sync, it all worked out.

Part of Robin's experience involved not having a plan. Many of us need to know exactly how to get to where we want to be. In most love spells, and especially in fertility, it is important to find your way intuitively, through your heart and absolutely not your head. You cannot think your way into having a baby. You can intellectually understand that you want one, but this isn't a rational process at all.

More involved spells can increase both the man's and the woman's fertile flow, but the most overlooked spell, and probably the most productive, is the spell for spaciousness around fertility. Most of the chapters in this book contain some spell for space. This is important to the spell process to avoid putting too much of your will into your magic, and to give the universe some room to work. You'll also find this spell useful if you are an immediate-gratification junkie. You must become accustomed to the waiting period, the gestation period, if you will, of the process of making a baby. Not only will you have to wait to find out if you've successfully conceived, but you will also have a nine-month waiting period before you meet your child. Get used to the mystery of life, and use a spell for spaciousness so that you don't drive yourself crazy with anticipation.

spell basics

♥

COLOR: Green

FLOWER: Sunflower or white geranium

HERBS: Any nuts or cones, cucumber, chamomile

CRYSTAL: Moonstone

DAY OF THE WEEK: Monday

TIME OF THE DAY: Fourth hour after sunset

TIME OF THE MONTH: Waxing Moon

FOODS: Bananas, cabbage, leafy vegetables

primary spell to
CONNECT TO THE
COSMIC FLOW

In the twilight of the day of a
new Moon:

Light a green candle,
place a white geranium next to it,
and place any combination of nuts in their shells and
pinecones in front of the candle.

SAY ALOUD:
In the flow of mystery,
under the power of the Moon,
we acknowledge that we are a perfect part
of the Divine Plan.
We affirm that in accordance with the Universe
we connect with the flow of energy, love, and fruitfulness,
and we release fear, judgment, and negativity
in order to create sacred space for life.
We know this to be true and bear witness
to it with pure intention, and say
So be it.
And so it is.

Water the geranium.

Use the nuts and cones in a fertility charm
and let the candle burn to the end.

charm to
INCREASE FERTILITY

On a Thursday during a waxing Moon,
in the fifth hour of darkness:

Light a green candle.

Combine at least three of these ingredients in a natural vessel:
nuts in their shells
sunflower seeds
cucumber seeds
pinecone(s)
chamomile
rice grains
Add a drop of poppy or patchouly oil into the mix.

SAY ALOUD:
In the flow of all creation,
I honor my power of fertility with love and blessing and
ask that this be in accordance with the greater good.
I release this with love and say
So be it.
And so it is.

Blow out the candle and encase the charm contents in green
cotton, sewn together with white or yellow thread.

Carry it with you or keep it next to your bed.

spell to induce
FERTILE PERIODS

On a Monday during a waxing Moon,
in the third hour of darkness:

Light a green candle and a white candle.
Place a bowl of hazelnuts and a vase with daffodils,
sunflowers, or cyclamen in front of the candles.

Hold an egg in one hand, an acorn in the other.
Sit before the candle. Close your eyes.

Breathe in deeply. Feel your breath
enter into your whole body, all the way to your ovaries.
Feel the energy of your body.

SAY ALOUD:
I honor the power of my body
to produce life and to foster healthy growth of a new being.
I am in the flow of the Universe and know that this is done
within the greater good. I love and bless my birth-giving
process, and ask the Goddess to touch me with
her fertility. I release this with love, saying
So be it.
And so it is.

spell to induce
POTENT SPERM

On a Tuesday during a waxing Moon,
in the fourth hour of darkness:

Light a green candle and a yellow candle.
Put a bowl of water, a bunch of grapes, and a mandrake
root in front of the candles.

Hold a date in your right hand.
Hold your hand open with the date in your palm.
Circling the candles four times, clockwise.

SAY ALOUD:
I gather the forces of the Universe to
empower myself with life-giving potency. I ask the Goddess
to aid me in this power, and I ask that this be
done for the greater good.
I own this power and use it for the purposes of Divine Love.
So be it.
And so it is.

Place the date in your left hand and eat it.
Blow out the candles.

Eat the grapes at your leisure.
Use the water to nourish your plants or yard.
Carry the root with you.

spell for
SPACIOUSNESS AROUND FERTILITY

On a Thursday during a waxing Moon,
in the first hour of darkness:

Light a purple candle and a green candle.
Place in front of the candles a bowl of water, some
nuts in their shells, and some tea leaves.

SAY ALOUD:
With the power of the elements
and the universal energy,
I gather the space and depth and breadth
that is appropriate for this time.
I honor and allow the process of conception
to know its own place and time.
I release my will and
ask that the will of the Universe be done.
So be it.
And so it is.

Blow out the candles.

Use the water, the nuts, and the tea to
nourish the earth by putting them in
plants or in the earth outside.

SIX

SPELLS
FOR
REIGNITING
PASSION

It happens to all relationships—that stagnant, inert sensation that makes you feel as if all the fire and passion have gone. Relationships have their own rhythm, their own seasons, and that full bloom of first love cannot be sustained any more than you can make the finest spring day last forever. After that rush of romance, there is a riper time of love, like summer, when consistently agreeable weather makes almost any part of life tolerable. Following that, the harvest-time in a relationship can seem like the beginning of the end, when mutual stimulation can be replaced by complacency. This is when the feeling of being taken for granted may surface instead of the comfortable feeling of being relied upon. This grayness can lead to a time devoid of passion, the winter of relationships.

For some, this cycle is natural, even not really noticeable, and the bloom of spring can spark dull fires to full flame without effort. It just takes time, patience, and a compatible cycle between you and your lover.

Many times, however, problems arise, making it difficult to find those dormant flames. Often this is a simple matter of attention. You or your lover, or both of you at once, aren't putting energy into your relationship. This is fairly easy to resolve with spell casting. It is simply a matter of bringing the imbalance to your attention and then stoking the fires.

There are situations, though, that can make this a more complicated, multi-stage process. These occur when you are not communicating with your lover, or worse, your lover is not communicating with you. This may frustrate you, because you have only limited influence over your lover's actions.

When you are the one who is holding back, you can do simple spells to break the ice and get yourself back into a more easygoing, spontaneous mood. When your lover is holding back, you can play with atmospheric spells to keep things light and to keep you tolerant, but ultimately it is up to your lover. If he or she won't give in to the passion you want eventually, you may have some choices to make. Don't think that these spells can make things all right again if the problems run deeper than ordinary relationship issues. If either of you is depressed or in mourning or experiencing some other form of emotional crisis, the flame of passion may not light. If you try to create passion where it cannot grow, you may end up feeling very frustrated and unfulfilled.

Simple sparks and aphrodisiacs

♥

Stacey and her husband, Peter, had been married for six years, with two children to show for it. Stacey works part time; her husband is a full-time manager at a manufacturing plant. They enjoy the craziness that the kids provide, and would admit without reservation that they have a good marriage. Stacey wasn't forthcoming with details, but let me know that she wasn't very happy with their passionate life—or, more accurately, the lack of passion in their marriage. She implied that while they were fairly active in bed, it just wasn't that interesting. She wanted to be more adventurous, but was not comfortable talking about it with Peter. Also, she didn't really know what to do about it. She was familiar with all the books about sex that are available these days, but she really didn't know what would be right for her, or what would be pleasing to Peter. While Stacey's problem was in part a lack of passionate interest, it was also partly a communications problem.

Stacey laughed when I offered her basic aphrodisiac advice, since it sounded so trite. The truth is that there is much in the old wives' tales, but you must go with what is instinctively right for you. Find a way to get the kids out of your hair for the time you have together. For atmosphere, red roses or red carnations are a good start, as well as candles of a certain scent. These trappings, combined with a spell to ignite old flames, are usually very successful. For Stacey, the spell reaction was twofold. First, Peter was surprised and touched that Stacey had made this effort, and said so. Stacey found her opening here to talk about her desires. The ice broke very easily and, according to a blushing Stacey, they reestablished their passionate connection to each other. She did underline the importance of keeping the children out of the way, however. She claims that as much as she loves them, the attention they demanded kept her fires low.

Some couples openly discuss their wavering libidos, and try to regrow their passions together. You can have fun with this by consciously consuming aphrodisiac foods, or what I call consumable love potions, together. Never slip a potion or concoction to someone without his or her permission. This process is only for mutually consenting adults; otherwise you've departed from the safety of white magic and have entered less predictable and often dangerous ground.

After casting a spell or two for atmosphere and/or firing the passions, consume a meal of hors d'oeuvres with some of the ingredients listed, and see what happens.

Energetic practices
♥

Another way to increase passion is through energy-shifting spells. These are more classic spells and, with practice, can be done both before and during the process of lovemaking, for rather incredible results. Energetic influences from your spell can open up new depth and consequently new pleasure. Sometimes your practices stay the same, but are more intense and more satisfying. You do not need your partner's permission to do these spells, but you will need a partner who is emotionally open to your physical relationship. Tania, a lovely, earthy woman, told me of her success with energetic magic. She was having problems with her lover, Sam, who was going through a stressful time and had problems maintaining an erection. Their relationship was suffering from his self-directed anger, and things were going from bad to worse. They eventually had no sex at all. Tania did not like that one bit, and cast her spell for reigniting passions alongside a spell to create an occasion for an energy practice. She soon got her wish, when, after an uplifting movie and a relaxed dinner out, Sam himself initiated some cuddling with Tania. In these moments of intimacy, Tania silently cast her spell, sending energy from her heart through to her hands, and placing them on his heart center and, eventually, into her root chakra, the bottom of her pelvis. Sam responded without hesitation, and their physical connection was strong, ardent, and powerful. Their reconnection of passion bridged a new bond of understanding and support between them, and Tania, thrilled with her results, has continued exploring the possibilities of energy-shifting with Sam.

Casting glamours
♥

Casting glamours can also be done to heighten passions. Reminiscent of sexual role-playing games, casting a glamour can give you an aura that will be seen as new, intriguing, or more compelling than the way your partner now sees you. If you think you are being taken for granted, this is a way to draw attention to your specialness. If you want to improve your mystery, your intensity, or your power, casting a glamour can be helpful.

Cassie and her boyfriend, Kent, have lived together for eight years. They don't have children and don't plan to, and agree that, while they have a lifetime commitment to each other, they don't need to get married. They both think of marriage as a passion killer. They didn't count on time being another demon. While they both agree that their relationship is strong, both have admitted to looking at other people, thinking about what it might be like to sleep with someone else.

Cleverly, Cassie got Kent thinking about spell casting, which Kent found to be an interesting and seductive subject. He didn't want to participate in any spells, but told Cassie he didn't mind if she tried one or two out. Kent was not home when Cassie did the spell work—on a Tuesday, for the fire of Mars's day. She didn't tell him what she was going to do or when it was over, just so they wouldn't be self-conscious. In her spell, Cassie spun a glamour for herself; she amplified her energy to be more magnetic and seductive. The night after her spell, nothing happened. Nothing happened the next day, either, and life took Cassie's attention away from the spell. As often happens, the spell wove its magic when she stopped paying attention to it. The following Monday, both Kent and Cassie came home from work early and unexpectedly. With more time on their hands, they decided to go for a walk in the early evening, and had a drink at a local pub. In the dark on the way home, Kent took Cassie in his arms under a streetlamp and kissed her the way he had when they'd first dated, deeply, passionately, and urgently. Without dinner, without thought, they made love as soon as they got home. Cassie felt more sensual than she'd felt in a long time, and Kent confessed that he didn't realize how much fire there had been in him. Both are still enjoying the magic of the spell, and are now participating consciously and making their passions grow.

Not every relationship is ready for the fire to recommence, however. If you know, deep down, that you have to go through a quiet period, so be it. There are times for regenerative stillness. Love isn't measured by the number of times you make love. In fact, love is often most obvious during the fallow times, when pure faith and commitment show how deeply connected you are.

Reestablishing connections

♥

In dormant or fallow times, it can feel as if you don't have anything in common anymore. If you're feeling as though your lover were from another planet, you may need to cast some spells to get you both back into the flow of each other. In relationships, one is constantly balancing power, fear, joy, anger, and other emotions. Sometimes you hold the power, sometimes you're left holding the sadness. Your relationship is an entity unto itself, making it a third person, separate from you and your lover. When you both retreat into yourselves and no one is watering the relationship, you can and probably do have a problem in relating to each other, connecting with each other, and finding your passion as a couple.

Spells that open and renew connections are more powerful when done by both partners together, but this is not always possible. If you choose to initiate a spell for reconnection on your own, you must first identify any resentment or hostility you may feel regarding this spell. In other words, does it make you angry that you have to take control of the situation to get your relationship back on track? Do you harbor resentment that your lover isn't making this effort? If you find that you are at all angry, don't do this spell yet. You need to clear yourself of any negative energy because it will taint your spell and can cause backlash.

To clear yourself of negative energy, use the spell for clearing energy (see page 123) on a waning Moon, and then cast a spell for reestablishing connections when the Moon is new again.

Brook and her husband Ed were on the outs and had been for at least three months. Brook was angry at Ed for not taking more time for her and spending too much time working or "just loafing," as she called it. They had little sex life at all, since she'd refused his advances from her anger and isolation. Brook felt that she didn't want to leave him, but she didn't know if she loved him, either. Her anger was too strong. In her spell for clearing energy, Brook worked to release what she thought was her anger, but found that it was actually fear of being deserted. She hadn't realized how hurt she was since Ed hadn't taken any interest in her. After she cleared her anger, Ed could see her sadness, and she allowed it to be discussed. Even though Ed didn't feel there was a problem, he did want to work things out for Brook. He claimed to be open to more time together. Brook then cast her spell for reestablishing connections, unbeknownst to Ed.

The fine weather of spring seemed to cooperate with Brook's spell, and the barbecues, picnics, and tennis tournaments they were invited to pulled them together as a couple. Brook cast a glamour to entice amorous interest from Ed, and it worked in a very satisfying if unexpected way. Although her glamour was not intended for any-one else, Brook found herself being flirted with virtually everywhere they went. This lifted her ego and, of course, had the appropriate effect on Ed, a little jealousy. Eventually the rites of spring took hold of both of them, and they enjoyed the rebirth of their sensual life. Brook claims that her spell work gave their marriage a new lease on life. Even if Ed gets lazy now, she feels that she has the power to do something about it. Ed, however, has not yet returned to inertia. He has too much to do, socializing and enjoying his wife.

spell basics

♥

clearing spells

COLOR: White

FLOWER: Iris

HERB: Bay

CRYSTAL: Clear quartz

DAY OF THE WEEK: Monday

TIME OF THE DAY: First hour after sunset

TIME OF THE MONTH: Waning Moon

reigniting passion spells and charms

COLOR: Red

FLOWER: Violet with lavender or hibiscus

HERB: Rosemary

CRYSTAL: Ruby or garnet

DAY OF THE WEEK: Tuesday

TIME OF THE DAY: Fifth hour after sunset

TIME OF THE MONTH: Waxing Moon

primary spell
FOR REIGNITING PASSION

On a Tuesday during a waxing Moon,
in the fifth hour after sunset:

Light a red candle.
Place a glass of water next to the candle.
Place before the candle, in a natural vessel:
lavender
rosemary
violet
cinnamon
Dab the candle with vanilla and musk.

Focus your attention on your heart center.
Imagine energy drawing up through your body from the earth
and emanating from your heart center.

SAY ALOUD:
Our fire is passion, our water is lust,
The earth of our bodies melts in the air of our desires.
With the blessing of the Universe
I ask that infinite passions between us ignite.
So be it.
And so it is.

Blow out the candle, but save it for use in a romantic moment.
Drink the water.

Place the herbs discreetly in your bedroom.

spell for
CLEARING ENERGY*

On a Monday during a waning Moon,
in the first hour after sunset:

Light a white candle.
Place an iris in a vase with water next to the candle.
Place a bay leaf before the candle.

SAY ALOUD:
I ask that space be cleared and open
for our love to reconnect.
I allow the obstacles and impasses to slowly diminish,
and I breathe through the fear I hold during this time.
I ask the forces of the elements,
the Goddess Venus, and my heart's desire to guide me.
I ask that this be done for the greater good.
So be it.
And so it is.

Burn the bay leaf in the flame of the candle.
Blow the candle out.

Do not use this candle
for romantic situations.

*Recommended for use as another Primary Spell.

simple
SPARKS AND
APHRODISIACS

(These tools can be used at any time, during any Moon phase.)

atmosphere enhancers

red clothing

garnets

rubies

incense of cinnamon, jasmine, rose, sandalwood,
ylang-ylang, fire (candles)

red flowers (especially roses and carnations)

aphrodisiacs

Enjoy whatever combination of the following that you desire.

licorice

onion

garlic

cashews

dill

celery

asparagus

eggs

chick-peas

saffron

artichokes

carrots

endive

honey

mint

ginseng

avocado

chocolate

to entice a woman
Wear the scent of
bay, musk, or stephanotis.

to entice a man
Wear the scent of
jasmine, lavender, gardenia, or musk.

energetic practices
FOR PASSION

(These practices can be done during any Moon phase,
but work best if done after the Primary Spell.)

Within twenty-four hours of the time you wish to
make love, sit before a red candle with a red rose in water.
Breathe deeply, in and out, slowly quieting your body.
Concentrate on your heart center.
Breathe red light into your heart center.
Visualize this red energy penetrating your heart
and flowing into your hands.
Allow the energy also to flow into your pelvis.
Keep this vision going, breathing in and out
and allowing the red energy to pulse into your hands and pelvis.

Allow the energy to stay in your body.

SAY ALOUD:
Within the mystery of the elements
I accept the fire of passion,
the pool of my love,
the atmospere of romance,
in the earth of my body.
I hold this energy and draw on it in a physical
manifestation of love.
With gratitude for this pleasure, I say
So be it.
And so it is.

Use the candle and the rose for atmosphere.

spell for
CASTING AN ENTICING GLAMOUR

Before your lover arrives:

Light at least four votive candles, pink or red.
Place lavender in four corners of the room.
Wear something red against your skin.
Place red flowers in a vase of water.

Sit in the room.
Close your eyes.
Breathe in and out of your heart center.

SAY ALOUD:
I gather the power of the elements
and ask that they join with me
in creating my beauty and desirability.
I release negativity and fear to create
space for the energy of passion and connection.

Imagine yourself in your most desirable vision.
Hold the vision. Be the vision.

SAY ALOUD:
I claim this energy as my own, and
delight in the passion that we create together.
So be it.
And so it is.

spell to
SHARE THE PASSION

On a Tuesday during a waxing Moon,
in the fifth hour of darkness:

Together, light two red candles
and two pink candles.
Touch each candle with the scent of
rose, lavender, or musk.

Give each other flowers:
violets
daisies
hibiscus

Give each other a drink of water.

Sit together before the flames.
Breathe in and out, quietly feeling your energies mingle.

SAY ALOUD TOGETHER:
We honor the fires of passion.
We welcome the lightness of air.
We enjoy the pleasures of the earth.
We drink the warmth of love.

Enjoy the evening.

spell to reestablish
CONNECTIONS

On a Monday during a waxing Moon,
in the first hour after sunset:

Light three candles, white, pink, and red.
Place a picture of your lover in front of the candles.
Place white daisies in a vase with water.

Stand before the candles.
Hold your open hands in front of you, palms up.

SAY ALOUD:
With the power of the Universe, an open heart and
an open hand, I call in the elements.
I affirm I reopen the connection
with _____,
and that we find our common path.
I offer my love and put forth respect for this process.
I ask that our love be reborn.
I say this for the greater good, and release it with
my blessing and say
So be it.
And so it is.

Allow the candles to burn until you
feel comfortable blowing them out.

SEVEN

SPELLS
FOR
LETTING
GO

Spells for letting go encompass different situations that you encounter when a relationship has come to its end. If you are the one who wants to break up, you will find success with spells to weaken the bindings of love and establish a compassionate path out of your relationship. If you are left by someone you love, you can find solace in spells to heal a broken heart. These spells will not bring a lover back, nor will they help you with revenge; the best use of these and any other spells is in healing. Do not add to the negative energy in this world. Help alleviate it.

The best thing about spells for letting go is that you can feel better for it. You don't have to go through a classic ugly breakup situation, with tears, accusations, and other unpleasantness. Instead you can weave protective energy around the two of you, so that you don't suffer unnecessary pain. You can go through the process with integrity, and not have some nasty karmic hiccup occur in your next relationship.

This may be news to you. There are actually ways to break up with a partner without causing and feeling untold grief. You may find that it takes courage, but, with a good spell, you'll have that taken care of.

This doesn't mean that there won't be pain, either. You will probably feel sadness or loss; it is only natural to feel pain when a relationship ends. But these spells can help keep you from making the pain worse, and possibly prevent bitter reprisals.

It is important to allow your negative feelings—fear, pain, anger—to surface. Those feelings are natural and important to your process. Please allow them. If you don't, you may have to wait a very long time to heal from the breakup, no matter who initiated it.

◆

Timing

♥

Contrary to spells that manifest love, those that are intended to diminish the connection between two people or sever ties are cast as the Moon fades, or wanes, after the full Moon until the Moon is new. As the Moon fades, so will your ties, your bond of energy, or whatever it is you want to let go of.

The most powerful banishing time is during the darkest sky, between the third quarter of the waning Moon until two days before the new Moon.

Do not cast manifesting love spells during your severing period. If you try to create new love in your life before the old one has faded properly, you could end up back with your former lover or, worse, with the same thing in a different package.

Natural resistance

♥

Even if you are the one initiating the breakup, you are bound to feel natural resistance to implementing it. It isn't a happy process on either end, but in order for you to "do the right thing," you are going to have to stick to the program for a while.

As mentioned above, there is going to be a certain amount of pain for you and your lover. This also demands patience from you. You can't just dump and run. The spell process needs time in which to work; the Cosmos does not take kindly to rush orders.

Patience, spaciousness, and gentleness are all important to letting go, regardless of who is doing the leaving.

◆

Spells for when you want to leave

♥

There are several steps you can take with spells for leaving. If you want a gentle, chivalrous parting, you can create spacious energy for the scene to play itself out, before you do a final spell to break ties altogether.

In casting certain banishing spells, you can loosen up the energy between you, to give more breathing space to your partnership, as a first step toward leaving. This can be done simply by changes in the atmosphere. My friend Dennis told me that just before he asked his girlfriend to move out, he followed the steps of the atmospheric spell. He commanded the atmosphere of his apartment to reflect his changing feelings. His girlfriend responded to the change in the atmosphere quite unconsciously; she began to criticize the coldness of his furniture, the inhospitable kitchen, and even the lack of heat from the radiators. Dennis was a bit naughty, too; knowing that she disliked the cold, he kept his heat turned lower than before. Eventually his girlfriend suggested they move to another place, and he took the opportunity to suggest she move on her own. There were tears on both sides, but the small atmospheric adjustment that Dennis did with his spell allowed the subject to come up naturally. As they parted, Dennis did a spell to clear the atmosphere, and carried a charm to help him readjust to his new single life.

You can take small steps, as Dennis did, to cautiously build up to a breakup, or, like Anita, you can do one large, all-purpose spell and see how it works. For Anita, who had been seriously dating Martin for eighteen months, there was a sense of urgency. She couldn't stand what she called the claustrophobia of their relationship. Martin was becoming more and more dependent on her for everything, and Anita finally couldn't take it anymore. To try to avoid devastating him, Anita decided to use a spell to give her the immediate space she needed without dropping him flat. Her spell for space and relaxing the ties between them was cast as the Moon was in its final third.

The evening after she cast the spell, she told Martin that she needed some time on her own to deal with some problems. Martin didn't need more than that to jump to the hysterical conclusion that they were breaking up, and Anita couldn't hide it, after all. They broke up that night, with tears, accusations, and some bitter barbs from Martin after too much wine. Still, the peace and calm after they parted left Anita knowing that it had happened the right way. Relief was what she felt, then a lingering sadness for the part of Martin she still loved. Martin had a few bad days, but within the week he apologized to Anita and they were able to end things on less dramatic terms.

These spells do not prevent heartbreak; they act more like "integrity insurance" so that you don't make false assumptions about other people's reactions and so that you can follow your own heart's desire without causing unnecessary pain.

One of the worst things that can happen in a breakup is for one partner to lie to the other. Many people believe that a simple lie is the best way to spare someone's feelings. This just isn't so. A spell can help you maintain your integrity and find a way out of a relationship without being hurtful. Leaving someone you have loved does not denigrate you or make you a bad person. However, you can attract negativity if you do not honor the other person within this time. Your honor and that of the other person depend a great deal on your clarity, integrity, and compassion.

Another useful tip for the spell you cast to break off a relationship is releasing your soon-to-be ex-lover as a whole. This may be difficult if you feel that he or she is not enough for you, or no longer satisfies your needs. If you take care not to diminish your partner in your eyes, in your belief, and hence in your spell, he or she will have an easier time healing, as will you. Don't forget, your relationship formed a bond to which both of you contributed. You don't need to take part of the other person with you when you want out, nor do you want your ex-partner limping around with less than he or she had when you started out.

There are no adverse effects of breakup spells except that you will no longer be part of a couple. If this is not what you want, you need to establish that now. You will also need to allow at least one full Moon cycle to pass before you even begin to think about attracting someone else. Emotional residue does not disappear with the person, and no amount of clearing the atmosphere will clear your heart. You must go through your own grieving process first, and learn to be on your own again before you get into the dating game again.

You may want to use the spells to mend a broken heart once you've implemented your breakup. Just because you wanted it to happen doesn't mean that you don't feel anything.

Breakup checklist

Before you cast the spell that can sever your ties to your current partner, check through these points, just to be sure that you are doing this for the right reasons.

1. Do you still love this person in a romantic/sexual fashion?
2. Do you really hope that your lover will come back to you a changed person from this split?
3. Are you hoping that the spell will create a way to communicate your unhappiness without causing a true breakup?

If you have answered *yes* to any of these questions, look more carefully at your intention. Are you trying to break up simply to draw attention to your own problems? If you harbor some belief that things can work out somehow, your spell will be affected. It would be better to be in a cleaner frame of mind, when you are certain that you can live without this person, and that you sincerely want to. In other words, leave for the right reasons, not the wrong ones.

Some common wrong reasons to leave

1. You are angry at something your lover did or said.

Leaving in anger is going to make it hard on the healing process. Let your anger settle, and if you then find that what has transpired is unforgivable or insurmountable, you can leave with more integrity. Anger can rob you of the power of saying what you want.

2. You think the grass is greener on the single side of life.

Try a spell for spaciousness, as Lanie did. You could try a separation to experiment with the single life. If you find that you are having a better time away from your lover, so be it. Cast your severing spell. It is a matter of overcoming your fantasy of what it is like to be on your own. For some, the fantasy is much better than the reality.

3. Your relationship is going through some troubled times, and you don't want to work it out.

Anyone who has been in a long-term relationship will tell you that there are times when you just wish you could get out, and that it's too much work. It happens. Relationships can go through periods that seem endlessly incompatible. Such a period can signal the end of the relationship, or it can be an obstacle that will eventually bring you together more intimately. If your relationship is troubled and you don't take a stab at working it out, you will only go to another one in which a similar problem will occur. You have to try, sometime. It may not work out, but you have to try. Once you try to work things out, if your relationship can't be mended, cast your spell to break up.

One last look in the mirror

♥

Before you sever the ties, look once more into the mirror of your relationship. Our relationships with other people tell us a lot about ourselves. There may be something here for you to learn.

If you are tired of an aspect of your lover, check to see if you share this trait. Irresponsible? Depressed? Critical? These characteristics in your lover may show you something about yourself. Maybe you provoke this behavior because you are deficient in it, or because you deny it in yourself. Maybe you've grown out of this need. Take stock of the underlying issues of your need to break up and learn from them. Otherwise you might have to go through it all again with someone else.

Perhaps not?

♥

If you feel there is some life left in your relationship, see the spells for commitment described on pages 95 to 96. You may be able to resolve things without going all the way into a breakup.

Spells to mend a broken heart when you've been left

♥

Most of us agree that it is easier to be the one to leave than it is to be the one who got left. It is often a nasty shock, a surprise, and something you can't really prepare for at all. Spells come in very well here, to help to heal the gap in your life, to bridge the sadness, to ease your transition into a new way of life.

Paul Simon's song "Graceland" sums up the initial feeling that accompanies a breakup:

> . . . losing love is like a window in your heart, everybody
> sees you blown apart, everybody hears the wind blow . . .

Spells for mending aren't difficult, but you must know that you will have to feel the pain of the separation, regardless of your spell. The spell is to ensure sound healing, not to anesthetize your emotions so you don't have to feel anything.

When Sara's boyfriend of two years stopped calling her and let it be known through quietly aggressive actions that he didn't want to see her anymore, Sara couldn't believe it. There had been no discussions, no warnings that she could identify, no hints that things weren't going well. She described the feeling of being dropped as like being punched hard in the stomach. She felt the wind knocked out of her, her balance totally thrown off. She felt nothing but pain.

Her first reaction was to crawl into bed and cry herself to sleep. She woke up with the searing pain again, though, and took the day off from work. She spent the day calling her friends, telling them the news, and crying off and on. She tried calling her now ex-boyfriend, but he wouldn't take her calls, and she still didn't have a clue to why they had broken up.

Her instinct was to drink heavily, which she did to the extent that an ugly hangover the next day made her feel even worse than before. Then she tried eating a lot of chocolate and ice cream, which also made her feel worse. In her desperation to alleviate the pain of her new separation, she tried casting a spell for healing a broken heart. Her emotional balance was off, and she didn't feel comfortable casting a spell aloud, since she felt it would just make her cry. Instead, she made herself a charm to heal a broken heart. The charm helped her with the immediate pain of the moment, and she cast a healing spell a week later, when the Moon was waning.

Sara knew that quick results were unlikely, and that she'd have to wait at least a few months to heal before beginning to look for new love. The charm she made helped her through the worst moments, and the spell she cast kept her in a healing framework instead of a self-destructive one. She found that her life filled up with other things: her pottery class, some freelance work, and traveling. She also saw the movies she wanted to see without having to argue with someone, and she spent more time on her own, happily fixing up her house and working in her garden. Sara's heart still felt a few bad moments throughout the process, but the healing she needed occurred in a gentle, easy way.

Rory's girlfriend was also abrupt about ending their relationship. She left him a note one day saying that she'd met someone else but hoped they'd be friends one day. Rory was distraught, but instead of letting his emotions "get the better of him," as he put it, he started seeing other women. He asked out just about every available girl around him, but his main target was Katie, his ex-girlfriend's best friend. He convinced himself that Katie was really the right one for him, and that his previous girlfriend had been a mistake. Luckily, Katie didn't agree with him. She suspected that he was just trying to make his ex-girlfriend jealous by going out with her. Katie agreed to see him once, for lunch, the least romantic time of day.

Rory begged Katie to go out with him, but she refused, telling him that she wouldn't consider it until he'd allowed himself to heal for a while. Katie was a spell caster, and had made a little healing charm for Rory. She gave it to him, telling him it would help him heal his broken heart. Rory laughed but took the charm, wanting to indulge Katie. As soon as he realized that he wasn't going to change her mind, he started feeling sad. He spent some time alone. He felt pain, but not in a dark, self-indulgent way. He missed having someone to think about and love. Rory began enjoying life again soon afterward, and now claims that he's better off on his own for the time being.

Rory avoided a rebound relationship by finally allowing himself to feel the impact of his breakup. He now proudly admits that he has healed and that it wasn't so bad after all. His ego healed very quickly.

As the preceding examples illustrate, after the initial shock, the healing process begins.

The process of healing

♥

Many of you share the impatience of wanting to be "over it" right away. No one likes to feel pain, no one likes to feel lonely. The process of healing from a broken heart takes its own time, however. You cannot dictate how fast you'll begin feeling better.

You can make it easy on yourself, though, by working with the process of healing and letting yourself feel the gradual awakening of your romantic senses.

The loss of a lover is very painful, but in this pain there really is gain. This idea takes a little getting used to, but the process of healing actually increases your personal power, your magnetism, and your ability to attract and give love. By participating consciously in the process of healing from a broken heart, you are also healing pain in other parts of your life. Sometimes it helps if you have the input of a therapist or counselor while you heal. Spells are just fine for creating the energy behind the healing, but they can't dissolve old patterns or old wounds that may still be keeping you from manifesting the kind of love you eventually want to create.

You may want help in exploring why your lover let you go. When you lose a job, you usually have a good idea of why: layoffs, political changes, even just your own mistake. Unfortunately, in love, we don't always get an explanation. If you do examine why things didn't work out, you will heal faster and more powerfully. You may even see your own accountability. No one is to blame entirely; in some way you contributed to the breakup.

I recall a particularly nasty heartbreak I experienced. I was a human puddle, unable even to remember how it felt to feel good. I got through every day on sheer willpower, and kept to myself as much as possible. I had a good therapist who was helping me see my accountability for this broken relationship, in which I had placed all of my hopes and wishes for my own life on my ex-boyfriend. My friends expressed concern for me, but I wouldn't let them in, my sadness was so deep. I did enchant a small charm to mend my broken heart, and I asked for some distraction from my misery.

An old school chum called me out of the blue soon afterward, and, not knowing that I was going through a hard time, didn't treat me with kid gloves. She persuaded me to join her in her volunteer organization. It was the best thing I could have done. I put my energy into something worthwhile, and I was helping other people who were less fortunate than I. The relief from feeling only my own misery was enormous. I healed just fine, in about six months. In the meantime, I benefited from the experience.

You may not be happy about anything for a while. That's just the way losing love feels sometimes. I can't give you a spell to make it all better right away, or to bring back the lover who left you. The process of healing is quite individual. These spells can only help clear whatever path you need to pursue. For every waning Moon until you no longer feel you need it, cast these spells for cutting ties, banishing grief, or releasing yearning. With each Moon cycle, you will find that your energy lightens and reweaves itself into a new balance.

When you feel clean, you can go back to the Candy Store and shop around for a little light love. Part of the healing process is getting your feet wet again, so the final stage takes you back to spells for attraction. Just don't get too serious, too fast. Have a little fun first.

Ending the healing process
♥

Since these are spells of banishment rather than manifestation, you may not be absolutely sure when you have accomplished your healing. Sometimes the loss and pain simply fade gently, and it is difficult to pinpoint the day you began to feel better. You may still feel pangs of attachment if you come in contact with your ex-lover. This doesn't mean you haven't healed. Sometimes, in close relationships, your energies have mingled long enough to create a natural connection that never fades. This is perfectly okay, but it can trip you up just when you think you're over it.

The final spell of the healing process helps close the wound and cleanse whatever emotional residue may still exist. It is a finishing ritual, marking the end of the mourning and healing from your last relationship, and showing gratitude that you have come through it whole.

This is a ritual spell that may seem odd to you. You are giving gratitude for the gifts that you discovered while in the shadow of the breakup. I gave thanks for finding my volunteer work, because I discovered another way I could find joy that no one could take away from me. Dennis had his own living space back, and the delight of making a mess wherever he wanted. Rory, whose relationship with his girlfriend had been the world to him, gave thanks for finding that he could live on his own and that he had the strength and intelligence to do things for himself. You may be grateful for rediscovering friendships, for improving your own self-esteem, even for having the spare time to rent your favorite movies. It is only natural, too, to be grateful that you don't feel pain and loss anymore.

This ritual helps you consciously identify what your relationship gap was filled with, how your life changed, and how your power came back to you. Often this healing process prevents a recurrence of the same experience. It doesn't guarantee that you won't go through another breakup, but it will give you more strength and more tools to deal with it if it should happen.

After you're done
♥

Hooray! You can see the light of day, the world is your oyster, life is good. You may want to get back into the social scene and find love again, or, if you're typically skittish, you may just decide to stay out of it for a while.

You may do as you like, but I do want to encourage you to get back on that proverbial horse. Even after the healing of a breakup, you may want to stay on the bench and not reenter the game. You may not even realize it, but you could be just a little afraid of another bad experience. That's only normal. BUT. You're not going to live without companionship. You're a veteran. You know you can survive anything, after all.

Perhaps the worst side effect of a breakup is the unwillingness to risk love again. Living in fear of being hurt is not living at all, and it is certainly not loving. One of the best gifts you can give to anyone in the world is your own love, so don't be stingy. You have an unlimited supply of it.

You don't have to fall in love again right away. You can play, you can practice-date, you can flirt, you can dance with cowboys and saloon girls until you drop, but you don't have to commit to anyone.

Don't forget how to play, just because someone pushed you down on the playground. Eventually the wound heals and you're out there laughing again.

Reread chapter 3 if you're in need of a pep talk and some insight into the pleasures of playing.

spell basics

♥

These are the basic elements that contribute to healing spells. You can use any of them in your daily life, to remind you of your healing process and to magnify the healing energy of your spell.

COLOR: White

FLOWERS: White roses, red carnations

HERB: Balm of Gilead (buds)

CRYSTALS: White quartz, rose quartz, amethyst

DAY OF THE WEEK: Monday

TIME OF THE DAY: First hour of darkness

TIME OF THE MONTH: From the day after the full
Moon until the new Moon

spell for creating space
BETWEEN YOU AND YOUR LOVER

On a Thursday under a waning Moon,
in the third hour after sunset:

Light two candles, one white and one blue.
Nearby, place red carnations in a vase with water.
Hold an amethyst of any size in your hand.

Close your eyes, breathe deeply in and out.
Relax your body, holding the amethyst lightly.

Quietly visualize yourself, alone in this room.
Feel the space around you. Fill it with your own breath.

When you are ready, see your lover, off in the distance.
You may invite your lover to come closer
or go farther away.
When you see the distance you like,
send your breath through your heart center with love.
Seal this space with your blessing.

SAY ALOUD:
This is my peace, this is my love.
Bless this space for the greater good.
So be it.
And so it is.

Blow out the candles.

spell for a
GENTLE BREAKUP

On a Monday under a waning Moon,
in the fourth hour after darkness:

Place a vase of white roses in water
next to a white candle and a picture of your ex-lover to be.
(An item of a personal nature can be substituted for a photo.)
Light the candle and sit before it with
rose quartz in your hand.

Look into the picture.

SAY ALOUD:
The blessing of our love does not diminish with this change.
I release the bond between us gently,
and allow the love we share to transform.
I honor and bless the gifts you have given to me.
And I bless and release all that I offered to you.
With the soft support of Venus,
I release this relationship
and ask that pain, grief, and sadness be easily healed.
With this spell I sever our ties,
and release you, _____, whole unto yourself.
With heartfelt forgiveness for us both
I say
So be it.
And so it is.

charm to mend
A BROKEN HEART

On a Friday before the new Moon,
in the second hour of darkness:

Light a pink candle and a yellow candle.

Spread a white cotton cloth in front of you.
Place at least one pinch of each ingredient mentioned below on
a white cotton cloth.

SAY ALOUD:

BALM OF GILEAD:

my heart mends and my sadness wanes with the Moon.

ROSE PETALS:

my love is purified, strong, and whole.

LAVENDER:

I recognize that there is still much love around me.

Sew the edges of the cloth all around, using yellow thread.

SAY ALOUD:

I weave healing, light, and vitality
into this process.

As you cut the final thread after knotting it:

SAY ALOUD:

I seal this healing charm with love and bless it.
So be it.
And so it is.

spell for
GENERAL HEALING

On a Sunday under a waning Moon,
in the fourth hour of darkness:

Light a white candle, a blue candle,
and a purple candle.
Place a bowl of salt water next to the candles.

Place an amethyst of any size in front of you,
a rose quartz to your left,
clear quartz behind you,
and a stone of your choice to your right.

SAY ALOUD:
I ask fire, earth, air, and water
to aid me in my healing process.
I ask for gentle cleansing and healing from amethyst,
hopefulness and faith from rose quartz,
clarity and purity from clear crystal,
and the energy and insight to align with the
flow of right action for what is to come.
With the grace of the Universe, I ask for healing.
So be it.
And so it is.

Use the salt water to put out the candles, and dab
some on your heart center.

spell for clearing
NEGATIVE ENERGY

On a Saturday under a waning Moon,
in the third hour of darkness:

Light a white candle.
Place a bowl of salt water next to it.
Place some dried sage in a natural vessel
such as a shell.

Ignite the sage so that it smolders.
Take the smoking sage to each corner of the spaces
you wish to clear.

SAY ALOUD:
I ask the powers of Saturn and the Moon
to diminish and banish any negative energy and to
restore the flow of right action to my life.
I allow all emotion to flow gently and gracefully from me.
And with the blessing of the Universe
I say
So be it.
And so it is.

Douse the flames with salt water and dab some
on your heart center.

spell for severing
YEARNING, NEED, AND HABIT

On a Saturday under a waning Moon,
in the fifth hour of darkness:

Light a white candle.
Place a vase of red carnations next to it.
Place three small pieces of thread in front of the candle,
of any color other than black.

SAY ALOUD:
I ask the power of the Universe to
relieve me of my yearning.
As the air flows into breeze, so does my habit yield to change.
As an ember turns to ash, so does my need turn to spaciousness.
With water to cleanse and the earth to support me,
I cut my ties, I sever my bonds, I release my habit.
I ask that this be life-affirming,
and I declare this to be for the greater good.

Burn each thread in the flame of the candle.

SAY ALOUD:
I release these ties to the Universe with love and healing.
So be it.
And so it is.

spell to
END THE HEALING PROCESS

On a Sunday nearest the new Moon:

Light a pink and a white candle.
Place white and pink roses together in a vase with water, and
place rose quartz or amethyst in front of the flowers.
Fill a bowl with salt water and place it near the candle.

Stand before the flames
with your hands palm upward in front of you,
as if you were holding something.

SAY ALOUD:
I bless this healing process.
I have gratitude that my heart has mended
and that my pain has been transformed.
With the support of the elements, fire for purifying, earth
for health, air for understanding, and water for compassion,
I affirm that the mourning is over. I own what has come
and gone, and I turn now to what lies before me.
And I say
So be it.
And so it is.

Lift your hands over your head, as if tossing a ball in the air.
Blow out the candle.

AFTERWORD

If you have read and practiced the spells, or if you have just read enough to get a feel for spell casting, you have already increased your power and ability to influence events.

One mere spark of knowledge from this book can bring your intuitive knowledge to the surface. You have your own access to the ancient knowledge of magic; pay attention to it.

You may also begin to use these magic practices in other parts of your life. You may just be on your way to an illustrious spell-casting practice.

Good luck, and good magic!

APPENDIX

Charm making for beginners

Some of the spells in this book call for making charms, or talismans, which are objects that have been charged energetically to bring to you what you wish. Charms can be very powerful, but it is important that you follow instructions and use these objects only for their intended use. The charms you make are for you alone. The only charms that work well for other people are those for healing broken hearts. These, when they are made with compassion, can be very helpful to people in distress.

Charm-making spells enchant an object that you make. You may use any ordinary cloth and thread. You are instructed to place certain ingredients on the cloth and then sew it up. It is easiest to start with a circular piece of cloth; when it is time to stitch it up, sew along the perimeter of the cloth, an inch inside. This creates a drawstring, and you can cinch the thread tightly to make a little bag. Wrap the thread around the outer gathering and push the needle through the center before knotting it.

Do not use silk or nonbreathing fabrics for your charms. Cotton and wool work nicely.

Disposing of spell materials

Materials from spells that protect or sever

• All materials used for spells that sever ties, protect from negative energy, or heal wounds must be disposed of after their purpose has been fulfilled. It is best to dispose of these materials away from home, in a body of water, a trash can, or a fire.

• Specific to healing a broken heart, you may wish to wrap your materials in a shirt or something your ex-lover gave you (a letter will do), and throw it away too. This is an excellent protection against that old negativity creeping back into your life.

Materials from spells that attract or manifest

• You may save for future use some materials from spells that manifest positive energy. If you are uncomfortable with saving anything, throw it out.

• The only spell ingredients that don't have longevity are herbs. These should be thrown out or put in the soil of plants; this returns them to the earth.

• Gems can be cleared and used again for something else. To clear them, hold them in the smoke of smoldering sage, or soak them in salt water made from sea salt.

• Candles can be used for other spells, as long as you have a conscious intention for their next use. Clear them simply by blowing out the flame with the intention that your spell is complete. If you forget to clear them, they can carry with them the magic of the previous spell. This usually doesn't produce negative results, but it is always best to clear everything when you're done.

• Flowers can be allowed to wilt and die in their own time. Discard them when they are dead.

• Charms should be destroyed when they have served their purpose. It is best to create a new charm each time you need one. Discard them when they are no longer needed.

• Anything else you have used should be consciously cleared or returned to the earth. If you've used a photograph or personal effects of the people involved, you may want to release them from your spell simply by shaking them back into their original forms. You can shake a photograph like a fever thermometer to shake off your spell energy.

index